First published in Great Britain in 2011 by Kevin Mayhew Ltd
Buxhall, Stowmarket, Suffolk IP14 3BW
Tel: +44 (0) 1449 737978 Fax: +44 (0) 1449 737834
E-mail: info@kevinmayhewltd.com

www.kevinmayhew.com

9 8 7 6 5 4 3 2 1 0

ISBN 978 1 84867 353 3

Catalogue No. 1501267

Cover design by Rob Mortonson
© Image used under licence from Shutterstock Inc.

Project managed by Free Range Book Design & Production

Printed and bound in Great Britain

Contents

Appendices

'Education is always at the centre of society's attention, and the place of the Church in education has never been under so much scrutiny. Meanwhile the Church of England is saying that church schools are at the centre of its mission. John Cox's level-headed and informative book is therefore very timely and deserves to be widely used as a background to all that's emerging in contemporary debate. Read, mark, learn and inwardly digest – then take courage and get involved.'

The Right Reverend John Pritchard
Bishop of Oxford and Chairman of the Church of England Board of Education and National Society

'John Cox has written a book that will be of immense value to Governing Bodies, Boards of Education and Headteachers especially of church schools.

Three things mark this book out as a unique and timely contribution to the Christian education of children. First, it is grounded in clear, orthodox and practical theology. It explains why communicating the depths of the Christian tradition is so enriching for children.

Secondly, it is full of wise, practical advice and suggestions which are accessible and useful.

Thirdly it reflects the pastoral sensitivity and accumulated experience of its author acquired over many years as a Parish Priest, Cathedral Canon and Archdeacon.

This is a gem of a book, the best of Anglicanism and something for all the church schools in my own Diocese.'

The Right Reverend Tim Stevens
Bishop of Leicester

'A Secretary of State for Education once observed that in general, church schools shared a plus factor, if he knew what it was he would "bottle it". John Cox who was a highly respected and popular Diocesan Director of Education delves down into what should be really distinctive about the ethos of a church school, and of Church of England schools in particular. This is a timely and helpful book which will benefit all involved with church schools, but which also makes a fine contribution in support of what is offered in such schools.'

The Right Reverend Nigel Stock
Bishop of St Edmundsbury & Ipswich

Introduction

Over the past five years or so I have been involved in the appointment of quite a number of head teachers to church schools. As the representative of an Anglican Diocesan Board of Education I had an advisory role at the selection process similar to that of the Local Authority officer present. I did not have a vote when it came to the decision about candidates but I was given the opportunity to ask questions from a church perspective. I normally asked each candidate two questions.

The first concerned collective worship, the act of worship required by law each day in community as well as church schools. Head teachers have a responsibility for this. 'How,' I asked, 'would you recognise a good act of collective worship?' Most candidates made a fair job of answering this, although sometimes their answers were more about what makes for a good lesson than what comprises a good act of worship.

My second question was usually this: 'You are a candidate for headship in a church school. What do you consider to be distinctive about a church school?' I would watch the candidate's eyes. As often as not I saw a slight glazing and then a hint of fear. They would really have preferred I had not asked that question. There is a similar reaction when I ask governing bodies the same thing. And, to be fair, it is not the easiest of questions to answer.

The answers that did emerge were too often, although not of course always, somewhat vague, and can be unkindly summed up as 'A church school should be a place of caring and sharing.' If asked to elaborate, the candidate would typically say something about the importance of each individual, and how everyone's potential must be given a chance to blossom. Most of these interviews were for primary school headships.

This may be a bit of a caricature, but the fact is that such answers just will not do. There is, in my experience, virtually nothing distinctive about a church school wanting to take each child seriously as an individual, helping them to realise their potential. I have never discovered a community school that declares it does not take individuals seriously. As often as not the points made to support the distinctive nature of a church school are not distinctive at all. They are values, aspirations and attitudes shared by the vast majority of schools.

It might be claimed that, because in this country we have inherited a generally Christian culture, what was distinctively Christian has in fact simply become part of our common set of values. But such a view should not go unchallenged. The so-called Golden Rule of 'Doing unto others what you would have them do to you', or its negative form, 'Not doing to others what you would not want them to do to you', has its equivalent in Jesus' teaching: 'In everything do to others as you would have them do to you: for this is the law and the prophets' (Matthew 7:12). But the Rule is not distinctively Christian. And it certainly did not originate with the Christian religion, or with the Jewish.

Church schools' mission or ethos statements can also be correct but too vague to be helpful when they state that the school upholds Christian values. Even providing a list of general values such as kindness, goodness, truth and generosity does not go a lot further in answering the question about the distinctiveness of church schools. To explore what might constitute such a distinctiveness, if in fact it exists, it will be necessary to look at some history and theology, because church schools have to be put into a context of time and belief.

I should make it clear that I am writing from a Church of England perspective. As I shall occasionally indicate, the Roman Catholic

Church has a rather different viewpoint when it comes to church schools. I also want to make it clear that I am not talking about 'faith' schools. Such a phrase is used widely both by the media and by politicians and is usually intended to include Church of England schools. This is not helpful. Indeed, it can be positively misleading. Very broadly, this is because 'faith' schools, other than Church of England schools, are by and large set up with the aim to preserve particular faith positions and nurture the children and young people in that faith, be it Roman Catholic, Jewish or Islamic. Such schools are established primarily for the children of believers. This is not the case for the vast majority of Church of England schools. Indeed, I would argue that, where such nurturing is the primary purpose of a church school, there is a betrayal of certain aspects of the very distinctiveness that is to be found in Church of England schools. This will, I trust, become clearer as we proceed.

This book is not intended to be a crib for candidates for headship in church schools or to enable governors to answer the questions of awkward Directors of Education. Its purpose is to stimulate discussion among teachers, governors, clergy and church people about what they think church schools are really about. I hope it will help them to consider ways in which the distinctiveness they feel it is right to preserve and develop can be encouraged and lived out within the whole school community and used to enrich the educational experience of children and young people. It is for the pupils that the Church is in the business of education – not to fill pews, not to ensure the continuation of a piece of ecclesiastical empire, but because the Church believes it has something distinctive to offer for the way in which children and young people are encouraged and enabled to develop into maturing and fulfilled adults.

I would like to thank all those who have helped in making this book possible: all the church schools in Suffolk, my many colleagues among Diocesan Directors of Education and the Local Authority with whom

I have had endless conversations, and most importantly my colleagues in the St Edmundsbury and Ipswich Diocesan Board of Education, whose help and insights have been invaluable.

Biographical Note

On retiring as Archdeacon of Sudbury in 2006, John Cox was appointed as Diocesan Director of Education, initially as a temporary measure and then permanently, with responsibility for 91 Anglican church schools in the Diocese of St Edmundsbury and Ipswich. He now enjoys a 'second retirement' but retains an interest in schools, being chair of governors at a church-aided primary school, on the board of a church-controlled school and governor at a church academy high school.

ONE

Why church schools?

We were having quite a heated discussion about the rights and wrongs of the Church of England. 'And that's another thing,' he said, abruptly changing tack. 'I don't know why we've got all these church schools. A waste of money! We should put our energies into getting Christian teachers into state schools.' There are plenty of people who share that view.

It is important that the Church no longer speaks of vocation solely in terms of the call to ordination. Vocations fairs and conferences nowadays take a much broader view and include, among other things, opportunities for people to hear about the teaching profession. And few would argue that Christian teachers should teach only in church schools. There are many who feel that their vocation to teach includes involving themselves in community schools where they can be light and salt and yeast, not proselytising, but living out their faith in an everyday act of witness.

In the Dearing Report, *The Way Ahead: Church of England Schools in the New Millennium*,[1] it was recommended that dioceses and parishes should be urged repeatedly 'to put before people what it means to be a Christian teacher and, in appropriate cases, encourage a vocation to teach'. But that does not mean there is no place for church schools with Christians among the staff. To some extent it's

---

1   Church House Publishing, 2001.

a matter of history. We have church schools as a result of the way English society and the Church developed over the centuries. They are part of the nation's educational heritage and it is one the Church of England has every right to be proud of.

Early school provision

There is good reason for the claim that mass free education began with the foundation of the National Society for Promoting Religious Education in 1811. But it would be wrong to think that there was no free education or education for the poor prior to that date. Nor was such education entirely prompted from within the Church of England. Neither high motives nor great expertise marked out some of the early provision, such as Dame Schools. At their simplest they were little more than a childcare service, with a local woman taking in children for a small charge, teaching them rudimentary reading and writing, while carrying on with her daily chores around the house.

Public subscription supported the establishment of charity schools as early as the seventeenth century, notably in London and later in York. Although the education these offered was usually quite basic, they were not without their opponents, who regarded such schools as socially dangerous and their advocates as social radicals.

Sunday schools

Christian philanthropists and social reformers who took up the cause of prisoners, the mentally ill and the poor in general often saw the significance of education as a way of improving the lot of the deprived, among whom they worked. Those who sought to find ways of preventing crime, and not simply its punishment, were among those who also pioneered educational provision. One such person was the Gloucester newspaper proprietor Robert Raikes, whose social concern had originally taken him to the local prison with its associated poorhouse. The ills he witnessed there led him to believe that schooling could be the best way to break the cycle of poverty and crime. In an age when many children were sent out to work at any early age, schooling during the week was not a realistic option. So Raikes, with the help of the local curate, decided to establish a school that met on a Sunday. His first school, established in 1780 in the house of a Mrs Meredith, was for chimney sweeps, in the aptly named Sooty Alley, opposite the prison he had so frequently visited. There is little doubt that there was an evangelical motivation behind this as well as social. The crowds of young ruffians he saw running wild around the poorer areas of Gloucester on a Sunday certainly had no education, nor did they have the benefit of a Christian faith. Reading and writing might be an advantage for employment but it also meant the youngsters would be able to read the Bible and the Catechism. So it was that the Sunday school movement began and, publicised in Raikes' *Gloucester Journal*, it rapidly spread throughout the country. It has been estimated that within seven years nearly 250,000 children were being taught in Sunday schools, and by 1831 the number had increased to one and a quarter million. Twenty years later, three-quarters of all working-class children were attending such schools. In the north of England and in Wales, adults also often attended, and as late as the 1970s in Prescot, Lancashire, a Sunday school had 5- and 85-year-olds in its classes.

John Wesley saw the Sunday schools as possible nurseries for Christians, while William Fox, a Baptist draper from Cheapside, believed they offered a practical way of realising his dream for free education for the poor. In 1785 he established the Society for the Establishment and Support of Sunday Schools, later to become the Sunday School Union, attracting both Anglicans and Dissenters to its membership. Although Fox was able to encourage hundreds of churches to create Sunday schools, there is an irony in the fact that his own church in Prescot Street was less easily persuaded to do so and it wasn't until 1798 that it set up a school in Goodman's Fields. Children were supplied not only with spelling books and catechisms but also with ink and slates, and funds were created to provide clothing for the poorest children. To teach writing on a Sunday – the Lord's Day – was a matter of considerable controversy and there was a strong Sabbatarian movement against it. Employing teachers for the purpose was seen as a further desecration of the Sabbath. The Goodman's Fields school overcame this by holding writing classes for boys on a Monday evening.

It was evangelical Christians who showed a particular interest in Sunday schools and among these was Hannah More, a teacher, playwright and social pamphleteer. A highly intelligent and creative person, she was herself the daughter of a head teacher. Her older sisters, while still in their teens, had, in 1758, established a boarding school in Bristol for 'young ladies'. It proved very popular and Hannah soon joined them on the staff. Subsequently, a visit with William Wilberforce to the parish of Cheddar spurred Hannah to begin a Sunday school there in 1789. She described her visit in this way:

> we found more than 2,000 people in the parish, almost all very poor – no gentry, a dozen wealthy farmers, hard, brutal and ignorant . . . We went to every house in the place, and found every house a scene of the greatest vice and ignorance. We saw but one Bible in all the parish, and that was used to prop a flower-pot. No clergy man had resided in it for forty years. One rode over from Wells to preach once each Sunday. No sick were visited, and children were often buried without any funeral service.[2]

With people in the parish having been visited to gain support and potential students, the school was opened in a barn in 1789. A house

---

2   H. Thompson, *Life of Hannah More*, 1838.

was provided for a school mistress. Hannah was a refo
quite conservative about social order, later writing tra
counter what she saw as the dangerous radicalism of s
Thomas Paine. She was, however, appalled by the level of
ignorance she found and believed that the key factor wa
moral teaching and religious knowledge. Wanting her scho
to be both entertaining and varied, she planned lessons to
abilities of the pupils. She encouraged singing as a way to res
of energy and attention, and although initially the only readin
was of the Scriptures, she later wrote moral stories and poems t
the students had more than 'seditious or pornographic liter.
commercialism' to read. Some local farmers believed that such s
with their teaching of religion, would be bad for agricultu
Hannah herself did not teach writing, otherwise known as 'cyph
since she believed such accomplishments would breed seditio
give the lower classes ideas above their station. The French Revol
had made even reformers cautious of undermining the social ord

'The object of the schools was . . . to make honest and virtu
citizens.'[3] In an age of a harsh discipline, especially towards the you
she argued that it was possible to get the best out of children if th
affections 'were engaged by kindness'. There were also rewards:
encourage them by little bribes of a penny a chapter to get by hea
certain fundamental parts of Scripture . . . Once in every six to eigh
weeks I give a little gingerbread. Once a year I distribute little books
according to merit. Those who deserve most get a Bible.' Hannah,
however, persisted in a view of children, held by many evangelicals,
as beings of a 'corrupt nature and evil dispositions'. Not for her the
idea of childlike innocence.

Through her social and church connections in London as well as in
the West Country, Hannah helped to play a major part, along with

3   A. F. Young and E. T. Ashton, *British Social Work in the Nineteenth Century*, Routledge and Kegan
Paul, 1956.

obert Raikes, in not only spreading education among the poor but so introducing methods that made learning accessible and varied.

Lancaster schools

A different approach was advocated by the Quaker, Joseph Lancaster, son of a shopkeeper in Southwark, who opened a free elementary school in Borough Road, Southwark, in 1798. Pupils were rewarded for successfully passing on what they had learnt to another pupil, a process sometimes called monitorial or peer tutoring, designed to provide a cheap basic education with limited resources and few teachers. The system initially proved popular and in 1808 The Society for Promoting the Lancasterian System for the Education of the Poor was created. However, standards were generally low and children were subjected to a harsh discipline. While corporal punishment was officially rejected by Lancaster, children who misbehaved could find themselves put in a sack or hoisted above the classroom in a cage. In fact, Lancaster was eventually expelled from the Society, not just because of poor financial management but because he was discovered privately beating a number of boys. In 1814 the Society was renamed The British and Foreign School Society for the Education of the Labouring and Manufacturing Classes of Society of every Religious Persuasion, later to be called, simply, the British Schools.

The National Society for Promoting Religious Education

It was the early success of these schools that in part prompted members of the Church of England to found The National Society for the Education of the Poor in the Principles of the Established Church in 1811, later to be called the National Society for Promoting Religious Education. Credit for being the driving force behind the formation and work of the National Society is usually granted to Joshua Watson, but educationally it was Andrew Bell who had the more direct influence.

Bell was born in Aberdeen in 1753 and, after graduating from St Andrew's University in 1774, he spent seven years in Virginia, returning home to avoid involvement in the War of Independence. He was ordained in the Church of England in 1785 and served for ten years as a chaplain and lecturer to British regiments serving in Madras, before health problems forced his return to England. It was during his time in India that he developed his ideas for a system of 'mutual instruction'. The inspiration for Bell's approach came from his observation of Malabar children teaching others the alphabet by writing in the sand, and he adopted this method of instruction – later known as the 'Madras Method' – in the orphanage school of which he was superintendent, the number and quality of teachers there leaving much to be desired. Back in England, he published an account of his method, and the system was introduced into a number of schools during the late 1780s, including army schools and the Clergy Orphan Schools (beginning with St Botolph's, Aldgate).

Despite obvious similarities between the approaches of Lancaster and Bell, they appear to have 'discovered' their systems independently. However, there was not much love lost between them. Bell was fully committed to the Church of England and some of his supporters saw the growing number of schools adopting Lancaster's method as a dangerous increase in the influence of the non-conformist churches. An article in the *Edinburgh Review* by Sarah Trimmer, who had followed Bell's approach in educating her 12 children, spelt out this danger. The article prompted Bell to produce *A Sketch of a National Institution for the training up of the children of the Poor* (1808), a pamphlet in which he urged the Church of England to follow his methods in schools throughout the country.

Bell may have been unhappy with the tardy response from the Church in general but a meeting in 1811 at the home of Joshua Watson was to prove both decisive and significant in the development of mass education for the poor. Joshua, son of a London wine merchant and himself a successful partner in his father's firm, had come to Clapton earlier that year, living just five minutes' walk away from his brother's rectory in Hackney and close to the parish of their brother-in-law Henry Handley Norris, with whom Joshua was to be friends for over sixty years. Together they were part of an informal group known as the Hackney Phalanx, a High Church counterpart to the renowned group of evangelicals known as the Clapham Sect. It was at their meeting in Joshua's house that Watson, Norris and John Bowles JP, a lawyer and writer, took up the call from Bell's pamphlet and proposed the setting up of The National Society for the Education of the Poor.

The first meeting of the Society, chaired by the Archbishop of Canterbury, took place that October and set out its purpose: 'That the National Religion should be made the foundation of National Education, and should be the first and chief thing taught to the Poor, according to the excellent Liturgy and Catechism provided by our Church.' The objectives were 'to teach them [the poor] the doctrine of Religion according to the principles of the Established Church, and to train them to the performance of their religious duties by an early discipline' and, secondly, 'to communicate such knowledge and habits as are sufficient to guide them through life in their proper station'.[4] While the primary objective indicated the clear religious intent of the education offered, a certain amount of secular education was also envisaged and this was to be carried out in accordance with the principles laid down by Andrew Bell.

A hundred and fifty years later, in a lecture celebrating the founding of the Society, Canon Charles Smyth was to say this:

Regarded in the light of our modern educational system with all the resources of the community behind it, this may seem

---

4   *An oration delivered by Canon Charles Smyth, Fellow of Corpus Christi College, Cambridge, on the occasion of the 150th Anniversary of the Foundation of the Society, on the Twelfth of October Nineteen hundred and Sixty-one.*

very inadequate and unenlightened. But, regarded against the background of the widespread ignorance and brutality of the England of the Napoleonic Wars, it can be recognised as a heroic missionary enterprise, financed by private charity, and designed to illuminate the surrounding darkness and to rescue the children of the poor, particularly in the new industrial and manufacturing towns, from heathenism and barbarity.[5]

A further fifty years on, even that has a slightly archaic ring to it but the reality is that under the guidance and driving energy of Joshua Watson the National Society had by 1851 established over 17,000 schools throughout the country. Whereas in the British Schools religious instruction was non-denominational, the National Schools explicitly aimed to teach Anglican doctrine and practice, including learning the Catechism as published in the Book of Common Prayer (BCP, 1662).

It is possible therefore to see a number of distinct strands combining to bring about the creation of a mass education provision in the first three-quarters of the nineteenth century. There was the philanthropic concern for the poor no doubt linked with a desire to improve public morality and reduce crime. There was a religious concern to overcome the generally low level of religious knowledge and faith commitment. This was further fired by a rivalry between members of the Church of England and other denominations, with the established church anxious to ensure that the national religion was taught throughout the country. But alongside this obvious religious purpose there was also the desire, among at least some, to provide a mass education that would not only engage young people but also prove useful to them in terms of employment prospects.

The first quarter of the nineteenth century saw an increasing radicalism, which questioned the existence of an established church

5   *An Oration*, op. cit.

as having wealth and power but little use. 'But', according to Canon Smyth, 'at a moment when the Church of England, which was supposed to be so rotten and effete, was engaged upon the heroic and prodigious task of planting a church school in every parish in the land, you could not seriously pretend that it was doing nothing useful!'[6] This was in some degree recognised by the 'anti-clerical' Whig government when, in 1833, it voted for an annual grant of £20,000 to assist the Church in its educational endeavours.

Towards universal primary education

The rapid rise in the numbers of Sunday schools and National Schools in the first half of the nineteenth century might suggest a thirst for education but there was in fact comparatively little enthusiasm among the establishment for general education provided by the state. At the beginning of the century Samuel Whitbread had advocated making each parish responsible for the education of its children, initially with just two years for each child between the ages of 7 and 14. Like others, he saw education as a way of reducing crime, but his proposals were considered too expensive to be implemented. The prospect of children and young people being taken away from their manual work raised the possibility of their becoming dissatisfied with their lot.

Working-class families themselves, often heavily reliant upon the earnings of children, were not keen to lose such income for the sake of a limited education. Despite the efforts of social reformers to reduce the levels of child employment, the number of children actually employed continued to increase even after 1850.

The enthusiasm of church members to establish schools for the poor, so often seen as the spur to the provision of universal education, may have actually contributed to its delay. Efforts in the 1843 Factory

6   *An Oration*, op. cit.

Bill to ensure that all headmasters were members of the Church of England outraged non-conformists and Roman Catholics alike. The insistence that all children should be taught the Catechism and attend Sunday worship aroused opposition from other quarters. The increase in the Catholic population, especially from Ireland during the period of the Great Famine (1845–50), and the restoration of the Catholic hierarchy saw the founding of the Catholic Poor School Committee in 1847. Priority was given by the Catholic community to establishing schools even before churches could be afforded. Denominational rivalry together with antagonism between religious and secular thought, which was an increasing characteristic during the second half of the century, helped to ensure that secular education was slow in gaining popular appeal. From the liberal point of view the Church of England's determination to control educational provision only added to the problem. An increasing majority of non-conformists, allied with relatively independent observers, concluded that the best way to provide basic universal schooling was through non-sectarian education.

However, the agreed success of the voluntary schools and a general *laissez-faire* political approach discouraged government intervention. The increase of wealth and economic development on the back of the Industrial Revolution had a higher priority than the provision of universal education.

Nevertheless the voice of those advocating education for all continued to speak out and a number of factors gradually created an atmosphere within which that voice would be more readily heard. The Factory Acts, with their concern for the conditions of workers, also placed increasing restrictions upon the use of child labour, freeing them to take advantage of education on offer. The more developed technical education systems of other European countries was credited with their making increasing inroads into Britain's commercial and manufacturing supremacy. Education was also seen as the answer to the rising social unrest, pauperism and crime which threatened political stability in the second half of the century. The cost no longer appeared such a deterrent.

Greater democracy

There was also the extension of democracy. Lord Russell's attempts in 1860 to reduce the qualification for the (male) vote to property worth £10 had been blocked by the Prime Minister, Lord Palmerston, but when Gladstone became leader of the Liberal Party, he made it clear that he was in favour of increasing the number of people who could vote. The ruling party, the Conservatives, realised that should the Liberals gain power they would introduce a Reform Act to widen the franchise. Disraeli, leader of the House of Commons, did not wish the Conservatives to be seen to be anti-reform so proposed his own 'Reform Act', stealing the Liberals thunder by making it more far-reaching than their proposals had been. With Gladstone's support the Representation of the People Act (commonly known as the 'Second Reform Act') was passed in 1867 giving the vote to every male householder living in a borough, and to male lodgers paying £10 for unfurnished rooms. It also reduced the property threshold for those living in the counties and added approximately one and half million voters to the electorate. This meant that the vote was no longer totally in the hands of the middle and upper classes. The Chancellor of the Exchequer of the time, Robert Lowe, remarked that the government would now 'have to educate our masters'.

The 1870 Foster Act

The election of 1868 brought the Liberals into power and Gladstone appointed William Foster as Vice-President of the Committee of the Council on Education. It was Foster who had responsibility for drafting the famous Education Act of 1870 which bears his name and which introduced state education. The Act divided the country into about two and a half thousand school districts, each with its own School Board, including women, elected by the local ratepayers who were also allowed to be Board members. The Boards were charged with surveying the elementary schooling, provided then by the voluntary societies, including the Church of England. Where that provision fell short of the required number of school places for children between the ages of 5 and 12, the Boards had the power to build and maintain schools out of the rates. They also had the power to charge fees but were able to pay the fees of poor children, including those who attended church schools. This and the fact that schooling was still not universally compulsory angered some Liberal MPs and such pressure groups as the National Education League. Boards could ask Parliament for a bye-law to make schooling compulsory but by 1873 less than half of the population lived in districts where this was the case and it wasn't until 1880 that the League succeeded in its campaign to make education to the age of 10 compulsory for all. It took until 1891 before all elementary schooling was free. The government provided grants towards the capital cost of building new schools but church schools were also able to benefit from grants made available through the Boards. By 1880 between three and four thousand schools had either been built or taken over by School Boards, and by the time of the Balfour Education Act of 1902, when School Boards were replaced by Local Education Authorities, there were some 5,700 Board schools compared to 14,000 voluntary (mainly church) schools.

Under the Foster Act, religious teaching was still required in Board schools but it had to be non-denominational and parents had the right in both Board and church schools to withdraw their children from religious education. The struggle by the Church and others to maintain their control on education continued, in some localities delaying the creation of the Boards or diverting the school rate into church schools. In some areas there was a rush to build more Church of England (National) Schools to pre-empt the creation of Board schools, while at the same time many of the non-denominational 'British' schools were handed over to the Boards because they had become financially unviable.

The 1902 Balfour Act

The denominational rivalries which had, in so many ways, dogged the education debates and arguments leading up to the Foster Act burst into flame again with the Balfour Education Act of 1902. It took nearly sixty days of parliamentary debate to get the Act through and much of that time was devoted to religious clauses. There were heated objections to the use of state funds to support denominational schools, especially, but not exclusively, those established by the Roman Catholic Church, which had given an increasing emphasis to secondary education. Under the Act, existing grammar schools received subsidies as well as grants to make it possible for them to offer free places to poor but able children. Teachers were to be paid for by the state, and funds were to be made available to provide all schools with the necessary books and equipment.

Some School Boards had extended elementary education for the older and brighter, and created de facto secondary education. In London this had been challenged by T. Cockerton, the district auditor, as being an illegal use of the school rate, which was to be used for elementary education only, and his position was upheld by the courts right through to the House of Lords. The Balfour Act changed this. School Boards, which had magnified non-conformist influence, were abolished and replaced by Local Education Authorities (LEAs), with county authorities given the power to establish secondary schools and fee-paying grammar schools. Politically the Act was seen by Liberals, non-conformists and the Labour movement as a Conservative attempt to bolster church schools, which they favoured, even though the Board schools had been outperforming Anglican schools.

But the Act did also bring voluntary schools under some government restriction as well as provide them with funding. All non-religious education came under the control of the LEAs, and while it was possible for church schools to continue to offer denominational religious teaching they could only do this by paying for school buildings. No pupil or teacher was to be required to conform to religious belief or practice and, by and large, the Church of England schools respected this ruling. Roman Catholic schools enforced religious observance more strictly and a canon of 1917 expressly forbade Catholic parents from sending their children to non-Catholic schools on pain of excommunication.

There were also changes in teacher training, which was seen as vital for the general improvement of standards. Most teacher training colleges in the nineteenth century had been established by the churches. The Act gave LEAs the power to support teacher training places and this led to a decline in numbers going to denominational colleges. To assist them, the government attempted in 1906 to ensure that colleges wishing to receive government grants had to forgo their denominational places. Both the Church of England and the Roman Catholic Church protested and their colleges were allowed to recruit up to half of their numbers on denominational grounds.

The first half of the twentieth century largely saw a consolidation of the position established at its beginning with a gradual extension of secondary education, a rise in the school leaving age and with still one-third of children receiving their education in church schools. But inequalities in the system remained, and while free places in grammar schools had increased to almost a half by 1937 in reality many of these were not taken up because of the actual costs that faced poor families if a child gained a grammar school place. Only one-fifth of children received a formal education after the age of 14. Nor was it clear that the education provision was meeting the actual needs of the nation let alone of the individual.

The 1944 Butler Act

While the Second World War was still raging, the coalition government under Winston Churchill began to consider the structure for education in the post-war period. It was Rab Butler, Conservative Minister of Education, who was responsible for the Bill that came before Parliament and was to become the 1944 Education Act. It replaced all previous legislation.

One of its major thrusts was seen in the scope and nature of secondary education. The Act provided free secondary education for all pupils to the age of 15 with the intention of making it 16, although this was not realised until 1972. Following the recommendations of a report by Sir William Spens in 1938 there was strong guidance by the Ministry of Education that secondary schooling was to be delivered within a tripartite structure, i.e. grammar, secondary modern and secondary technical schools. Entry to a grammar school was on the basis of the so-called '11 plus' examination, aimed to distinguish those for whom an academic education was most suitable and university a realistic ambition. Secondary modern schools were aimed at those pupils who would attend four years of secondary education before entering employment. There was no external examination but a school leaving certificate was given on the completion of the four-year course. It was possible to choose to stay on for a fifth year. Less popular and far less in number were the technical schools entered at the age of 12 or 13 from a secondary modern school. Their curriculum was more closely linked to the worlds of commerce and industry but, in part because of the lack of well-qualified teachers, they did not prove to be very successful.

The tripartite structure is now widely seen as socially and educationally divisive but at the time it was part of a wider educational philosophy that sought to meet the needs, abilities and aptitudes of each child. And, in spite of the existence of the grammar schools with their academic emphasis, the Butler Act sought to create an education that met much more than academic needs. The Act states: 'it shall be the duty of the local education authority for every area, so far as the power extend, to continue towards the spiritual, mental and physical developments of the community'. Such developments for the community could not be met without education also being concerned about the 'spiritual, mental and physical' developments of the individual. Education was intended to be child-centred. In the opinion of David Bell, chief inspector of schools in a speech to celebrate the anniversary of the 1944 Act, it therefore shares features with the Every Child Matters agenda some sixty years later.

Collective worship

Bell also viewed the concern for 'spiritual development' as one of the greatest legacies of the Act. In Butler's time this would have been seen in fairly narrow terms, namely through the daily act of Christian worship, which the Act required of all schools, and Religious Instruction. This was not seen as a particularly contentious issue, certainly not in the way it would be today, when more than three-quarters of all schools fail to meet the requirement of the law for daily collective worship. But the law remains on the statute book and was made only more complex by the 1988 Education Reform Act, which added the requirement that collective worship should be wholly, or mainly, of a broadly Christian character. Despite the efforts of secularists and indeed some church people to change this element of the 1944 Act it is noticeable how reluctant successive governments have been to entertain such a change.

Aided or controlled

Another significant aspect of the 1944 Act was the opportunity for church schools to opt for voluntary aided or voluntary controlled status. Aided schools retained their right to appoint staff, to determine admission policies, to have a majority of foundation governors, to decide on the nature of the Religious Instruction syllabus (often provided by the diocese), and for collective worship to be Anglican in character (in Church of England schools). In return, the governors of voluntary aided schools were to make a contribution (originally 50 per cent) towards the cost of their buildings. By contrast the voluntary controlled schools lost the right to appoint staff and governors (apart from foundation governors) and to determine admission, and they had to offer non-denominational Religious Instruction as set out in a locally agreed syllabus. Worship continued to be Anglican according to the trust deeds of the school. To 'compensate' for the loss of these powers the state was to pay all costs, including for buildings.

While the Roman Catholic Church opted to go entirely down the voluntary aided route, many of the Church of England schools decided on controlled status. In part this was because for many of them their buildings were now old and in need of modernisation, repair or replacement, and neither parishes nor dioceses could afford the contribution to the building costs required of them. Though not true of all parts of the country, most dioceses, as a result of the 1944 Act, have many more controlled schools than they do aided. To this extent, while the 1944 Act retained the 'dual' system of state and voluntary education, there was a decline in the number of schools where the Anglican aspect was so clearly 'structured in'.

The framework for church schools set out in the 1944 Act has basically remained the same during the years since then. The way in which the Church views its schools and the way they see themselves has, however, varied over that period and is reflective of the confidence with which the Church sees its faith and role in society. The 1970s and early 80s was a period of considerable anxiety and uncertainty in the Church, in part financial, in part a matter of authority as it came to terms with the aftermath of the late 1960s. The Church was less confident too about its role in education, both in its relation to Local Authorities and the government and in terms of its willingness to speak with a distinctive voice. By the 1990s there was a resurgence of confidence, and with the approach of the new millennium the Archbishops' Council of the General Synod asked Lord Dearing to chair a Church Schools Review Group 'to advise on the achievements and future development of Church of England Schools. Its report, *The Way Ahead: Church of England Schools in the New Millennium* was published in 2001, and reflected its terms of reference, which saw church schools as standing at the centre of the Church's mission to the nation. The Review Group was asked to 'examine the case for strengthening their distinctiveness and the means by which this might be achieved'. But it saw the Church and state as partners: a partnership it not only welcomed but wished to develop as fundamental to its whole approach to education.

The decade since that report has seen an increase in the number of church secondary schools, including academies, which was one of the report's aims, but it has also seen a Church that is too often distracted by internal controversy. There is the challenge of an increasingly mixed society both culturally and in terms of faith. Secularism has found an increasingly strident and confrontational voice, and government commitment to the dual system has sometimes appeared ambivalent.

The movements that saw the Church involve itself in mass education, especially among the poor, had mixed religious, denominational and philanthropic motivation. Not all of it was high-minded or altruistic. But much was and, at its best, concern for others and not merely concern for the Church lay behind its educational work. As the established church, the Church of England no doubt had issues about the part education could play in conserving the establishment, but there was also a desire for radical action in the name of justice for the poor, working from the fact that Christians are not only there for others, as they seek to follow Jesus, the Man for Others, but are part of a Church that holds a deeply felt conviction about its care for all – the cure of souls. The parish system is a reflection and a spur for this, and the same has become true for the Church's role within the dual system of maintained schools. As a provider of schools, the Church seeks to make a distinctive contribution but also one that is accessible to all.

TWO

A matter of belief – God

Recently I attended an act of collective worship in a primary school. It was the first time the school had celebrated Holy Communion in the school and it had done so only after a considerable amount of thought, prayer and preparation. It was a joyful celebration and in a packed hall there was a real sense of worship and reverence. There was plenty of participation by the children, not only in leading prayers and bringing in the offertory but also in leading the singing and in presenting work they had done over the weeks in preparation for this day. I had to smile when it came to the words of one of the songs:

> Thank you for our school.
> Thank you for our school.
> Thank you for this special place,
> Our caring, sharing school.

For here was a school where what was special about it was much more than just caring and sharing. And this act of worship had demonstrated it. The service included a simple form of the creed:

> Do you believe in God the Father?
> **We believe and trust in Him.**
>
> Do you believe in Christ the Son?
> **We believe and trust in Him.**

Do you believe in the Holy Spirit?
We believe and trust in him.
We believe in God, Father, Son and Holy Spirit.

At the heart of what makes a school and its ethos distinctive lie beliefs. They don't have to be religious beliefs – they could be educational beliefs, moral beliefs, social beliefs. There is no such thing as a belief-neutral education. And in a church school the foundational beliefs are those of the Christian Church. They are distinctive.

Constantly I find myself wanting to say two things at once: to speak of what is distinctive but to balance that with the insistence upon the need for a school to be inclusive. In part this arises out of a fear that by stating a position that clearly relates to faith I will sound as though this is what I want to push down the throats of pupils and students or insist that they affirm. That is far from what I intend. But equally I believe it does no good at all to be mealy-mouthed about the faith that should inform the life of a church school. The faith should be real, should be communicated by word and action, should be joyful and confident even while it remains faith and not a guaranteed certainty. What is said and what is lived is an invitation to pupils and students to see if it makes sense for them, see if it does indeed make a difference to the way they view things and want their lives to be. It is an invitation and an opportunity, not an insistence or indoctrination. If they decline the invitation having given it sensible and proper examination, that is fair enough. And no one should be thought the less for that or for choosing a different faith upon which to base their lives.

That some respond to the invitation is a matter of delight but it is a kind of gracious bonus, the working of the Spirit that blows where it chooses but is not in our control. That all pupils will be at least better informed about the faith and less open to simplistic prejudice is certainly highly desirable. That an encounter with the Christian faith opens minds, extends tolerance and awakens a sense of the spiritual is surely good education if nothing else. Schools may be places of mission – indeed, in the words of a General Synod motion, 'at the heart of the Church's mission' – but that does not mean they are simply arenas for evangelism. They are places of service, of growth and development, of social and personal maturing in which young people are seen to be of far greater worth than simply potential pew fillers.

So having, I hope, made it clear that I believe our schools are not to be places for an insensitive proselytising zeal, I now want to go on to set out what I understand to be some of the distinctive Christian beliefs that should underpin our church schools.

In essence these come down to four:

• what we believe about God
• what we believe about being human
• what we believe about the world
• what we believe about the Church.

In this chapter we will look at some of the distinctive beliefs that a Christian has about God. The other three points will be considered in succeeding chapters.

The foundation of beliefs about the nature of God begins with the fact that Christians believe God exists. That he does so is neither self-evident nor open to the scientific method which some people assume to be the only basis upon which 'fact' can be established. Belief in the reality of God cannot be proven that way but that does not mean, as recent judgements in the Appeal Court would imply, that belief in the reality of God is irrational and simply subjective, especially if that means 'individualistic'. Nevertheless commitment to the reality of God is in the end a matter of faith, not of a guaranteed, provable certainty with knock-down arguments.

Belief in God is not, of course, the specifically distinctive nature of the Christian faith. Plenty of other faiths believe God exists or even that many gods exist. What is distinctive is what Christians believe is the nature of the God in whom they believe.

Traditional descriptions of God have been very much influenced by Greek philosophical thought and have spoken of God being all-powerful, all-knowing and present everywhere – in other words omnipotent, omniscient and omnipresent.

Omnipotent

Christians certainly believe God has power and that he is more powerful than anyone or anything else in creation. If he were not then that other power would have power over God and in that sense God would not be God. But this does not mean that God can do everything, or that he always reserves all power to himself. God cannot do those things that are contrary to his basic nature, and there is a sense in which God seems to give his power away, making himself vulnerable. And he does so by choice, not because he is 'forced' to. His power is in this sense restricted both by his nature and by his choice.

As we shall see when we come to look at God as love, God cannot go against his own loving nature. He cannot act in unloving ways. His power is thus determined, as is all else about God, by this basic characteristic of his nature – love.

It also seems that God chooses not to use all his power all the time. He constrains his power for the sake of what he sees as a greater good. He risks being rejected by giving human beings the freedom of choice. He has taken the 'long way round' by creating a universe in which our maturing into fully responsive men and women happens without coercion but by invitation. In the cross of Jesus, God is seen most clearly to be 'handing himself over' to the will of others – endangering himself to bring about their greater good. The God of power offers himself – makes sacrifice.

Power and its use, particularly personal power, are important issues within a school and lie beneath such questions as anti-bullying policies, sexual harassment, attitudes to the vulnerable, knowledge as power, etc. They are also clearly linked with matters of authority – its use and its abuse.

Omniscient

God, it is believed, also knows all that there is to know. He is the source of all there is and all truth 'resides' in him. There have been times, and indeed it is still true, when the Christian Church has resisted the insights of disciplines other than theology and spirituality. One only has to think of the way the insights of Galileo and Darwin were opposed in their day not just by other scientists but by the Church. If God is the God of all truth, faith has ultimately nothing to fear from the truth disclosed by science or by anything else. Of course hypotheses need testing with rigour but opposition from a closed dogmatism does the God of truth no favours. Indeed, it arises from a form of blasphemy.

Schools should be places where truth matters as a moral issue – telling the truth rather than lies. But they should also be places where there is a robust and imaginative search for the way things really are and the way they interrelate – physically, morally, emotionally, aesthetically, socially, etc.

There may be a case for some aspects of subjects to be taught as discrete disciplines (especially at secondary level) but truth is seldom fully uncovered in subject-narrowed confines. Academic disciplines

– and this includes religion or theology – are tools for discovering truth in certain ways, they aren't themselves the truth. The more creative curriculum many schools are now pursuing is one way in which this wider understanding works out in practice. Not only learning skills are transferable across subject areas, often extending them – the same is true for truth. From different perspectives a fuller picture of the way things really are becomes apparent. Christians should be delighted by truth wherever it is found – not try to confine it.

Omnipresent

Imagery regarding God has often placed him in specific spatial terms, most obviously 'up in heaven'. At a simplistic level this has been taken literally to mean above the clouds, although space travel and popular astronomy have helped to expose the shortcomings of such a literal understanding. Yuri Gagarin, the first man in space, confidently claimed that there was no God since he had not found him above the clouds. 'God above', 'heaven up there', are better understood as metaphors and imagery helping us to express our sense of the majesty and grandeur of God, his otherness. Seeking to express truths that were lost in the picture of 'God in the sky' and 'God out there', theology in the last century tended to emphasise the God at the heart of all things, God the 'Ground of being'. God's place shifted from 'out there' to within – within the very nature of the created order itself and within the human spirit. This pendulum swing merely demonstrates the failure of any description of God to be complete and adequate. God within is no more an exhaustive description than God out there. The God of everywhere seeks to express the understanding that there is nowhere where God is not. Psalm 139 (see especially verses 1-11) conveys this with a haunting poetic beauty. But if God is everywhere this demands of us a reverence for everything that is, for the whole of God's creation, for the physical world as well as the personal. Christians believe that God is in all things and all things are in God but that he is also greater than the sum of all creation. Theologians have coined the term panentheism to describe this, distinguishing it from pantheism, which says that all things make up God.

God calls us to 'reverence' all of the created order and this will have an impact on the way a school considers not only individuals (made in the image of God and 'temples of the Holy Spirit') but also questions regarding the environment, ecology and the physical order. (See also, below: 'Creation and purpose' and 'A good creation?')

Love

What is most powerfully distinctive about God for the Christian is declared in the statement 'God is love' (1 John 4:8). It is love, more than power or knowledge, that distinguishes the nature of God. It is why I said earlier that God is powerful but cannot do everything. He cannot go against his own nature and therefore he cannot do what is not loving. To use the word 'love' about the very nature of God is fundamental to Christian faith but it is a word used so widely these days that without qualification it could be misleading. People happily say they love their dog, a favourite pop song, ice-cream or Boston in the Fall, as well as parents, spouses and partners, their best friend. Love can be manipulative and even be made the claimed basis for abuse.

The love that is meant when talking about God as love is outgoing, self-giving love. It is not calculating or self-concerned. It is generous and gracious, always adding to the worth of the beloved, never detracting from it. It is what we like to think we mean by love at its best. To say that God is love means that he is in his very nature outgoing, unself-regarding, worth-giving, generous and gracious. It is the love that we see taught and revealed in the life and words of Jesus.

Relationship

At its heart, love is a term that speaks of relationship. Love always has both subject and object – the one who loves and that which is loved. It does not make sense otherwise. This means that speaking about God as love must mean that at the heart of God there is relationship. This is at least part of what the rather strange and mathematically difficult doctrine of the Trinity (God is three and God is one) is trying to convey. It is indicating that even before there was the created order which could be loved, God already loved. There is love at the centre of God's being: the love of the Father for the Son, the power of that love expressed by the person of the Holy Spirit. But it is not simply self-love: God loving himself. The distinction of the persons of the Trinity (Father, Son and Holy Spirit) speaks of a relationship that is outgoing. The unity of the Trinity (one in three and three in one) seeks to safeguard the idea that there is only one God, not a committee of three! There is only one love, one loving. Language at such points struggles to convey what is believed and can only do its best. It will never be adequate. When we have made every effort to be as clear as we can, as true as we can to what God has revealed of himself, the fact remains that the nature of God is mystery and all our statements are less than the full truth.

Church schools should, above all else, be places where relationships prosper, are nurtured, are encouraged to mature with wisdom, are cherished when under threat or are broken. Relationships within the whole learning community are important not only between children, but also between children and staff, staff and staff, staff and parents, staff, parents and governors.

The Christian doctrine of the Trinity is distinctive and is not shared, for example, by Muslims. It seeks to encapsulate what it is believed God has revealed of himself and what is true of the Christian experience of God. At its heart it speaks of God who is 'relational', and key to the understanding of God is the person of Jesus. This is why the story of Jesus is so important.

Creation and purpose

That outgoing love which is the mark of God's very being is what 'motivated' and drives creation. Outgoing love seeks to express itself and to extend the 'sphere' of relationships. So God creates. The Christian does not accept that it was sheer chance that brought the universe(s) into being. It is the result of outgoing love, a love that is not pointless but has a purpose. God did not arbitrarily set creation on its way as some kind of divine whim. He has a purpose for his creation and that purpose shaped the form creation has taken and the rules that govern it, what some might describe as the laws of nature.

Such suggestions are hotly contested these days, not least by atheistic scientists and articulate secularists who attack what they see as obscurantist and dangerous views. Too often their arguments seem to be aimed at a comparatively small percentage of Christians – namely those who resist the insights of science when it comes to the age of the universe, and who give a literal interpretation to the creation accounts in the book of Genesis. Such people are often called 'creationists'. More liberal theology would certainly resist the 'timetable' for creation that such fundamentalists set out, and would wish to modify some of their ideas regarding the way in which God 'directs' his creation. But that does not mean that 'mainstream' theology and Christian thinking should thereby abandon the belief that God is purposeful in his creating. That the universe is the result of God's creative purpose also has implications for the way we view our world and how we should behave in relation to it. More will be said about that in a later chapter.

Incarnation and involvement

The God who is purposeful is also the God who gets involved. This is not self-evident. There have been plenty of Christians who have found it difficult to see where God is actively involved in our world today. That he created the universe in the first instance is not doubted, setting its direction and establishing the way it works. But, some have suggested, that is where God's responsibility and involvement ended. Such a view was popular in the eighteenth century, when there was a great interest in new mechanical inventions. Intricate machinery was seen as a model for the way things in general worked. The universe was thought of as a great machine, as delicate and intricate as a watch, with God as the watchmaker. He had made the 'watch', wound it up, set it going and then sat back, leaving it to its own regular devices.

Such a view, however, did not adequately capture what the Scriptures and years of tradition said about God. It ignored a core factor in the gospel account – namely that in Jesus God has been intimately involved in this world and that such intimacy is in fact typical of God's loving concern for all he has made. Far from winding the universe up and leaving it to its own devices, God commits himself to it 'from within'.

Jesus is pivotal to our understanding not only of God but also of what it is to be human, for in him, Christians believe, God has entered the human condition to be born as one of us, subject to the rigours of life, physical, mental and moral.

Forgiving and transforming

It is sometimes argued that this is the best of all possible worlds. Even if that is true we know from our own experience that it is not a perfect world, if by perfect we mean in total harmony, without fault, unblemished. We only have to look into our own hearts to recognise that all is not well – all the time. Physically there are flaws and, even more significantly, the same is true morally. Without beating ourselves up about it, the fact is human beings do wrong. In religious language, they sin. And sin is not simply that we do things that hurt others but that we outrage the moral order – our sinning outrages God. This moral failure is universally recognised and different religions seek to show the ways in which they believe it can be dealt with.

For the Christian this issue lies at the heart of the gospel: the moral dilemma has been solved. There is good news for the human condition. God has dealt with sin. He has shown this through the cross of Jesus Christ. There is mercy and forgiveness offered to all. God, as it were, has taken upon himself to solve the problem that on its own humanity cannot – that is what the cross demonstrates and effects. And this is distinctive in Christian belief. The God of love and justice is a God of mercy and compassion – he forgives, he goes out of his way to find the lost sheep, he welcomes the prodigal back with open arms. Such forgiveness does not merely leave the sinner with the slate wiped cleaned, but also works, through the power of the Holy Spirit, to transform the sinner. There is hope not only for reconciliation between the grieved parties but also for lives made new. What is destructive can be changed. The life of death becomes resurrection life. It is the work of God, his grace, his spirit working in us for now and for our eternal destiny. It is salvation – a word that also means wholeness. Through Christ the broken can become whole, the dis-eased become healthy, the morally dead become alive, the sinner be saved. Such language can sound highfalutin but it has serious and joyful repercussions for the way we handle failure and understand forgiveness in our schools.

The Christian beliefs about God, for all their theological formulation, are not about abstractions; they are first and foremost about relationships – and both the Old and New Testaments are a treasure house of the story of God's relationship with his world, his people and all humanity.

The story of God's dealings with his people and the world, and the beliefs expressed through that story, form the basis for the distinctive ethos of church schools.

THREE

A matter of belief – being human

Back in the 1960s the principal of my theological college obviously believed in lifelong learning. When I was about to leave college he asked me what ongoing theological study I would be doing. 'Christology,' I replied after only a short pause for thought. It seemed to satisfy him, it being a suitably erudite kind of answer. But I meant it, not because I considered myself erudite or because I wanted to do a lot of academic study but because I felt the really important issue for a Christian, especially one who was going to be ordained, was the question (actually three questions) what do we believe about God, what do we believe about being human and how are the two related? Theologically this is what Christology is about – focused upon the exploration of what we understand by saying Jesus is both man and God. From a religious point of view I was committed to the belief that it is in the story of Jesus that we have both a unique insight and the fullest clues (revelation) about the nature of God and the nature of being human. This is why the importance of the story of Jesus is repeatedly mentioned in this book. If we are to discover what is distinctive about the beliefs that underpin the values and ethos of our church schools then we cannot, must not, ignore the story of Jesus.

But a commitment to Jesus does not mean that there are no truths to be discovered and explored apart from those we find in the pages of Scripture and the faith of the Church. As indicated in the last chapter, if God is the God of all truth then we should seek wide and far, delighting in the multiplicity of disciplines that help us to understand ourselves better. The intricacies of genetics and insights of sociology, the discoveries of neurologists and creations of artists, are all paths to be explored with delight and critical awareness. Delight because truth should expand our understanding, and critical because no insight has all the truth and some avenues may prove to be cul-de-sacs.

As has often been said, many of the paths of knowledge, particularly those associated with the sciences, have much to tell us about the 'how' of things: how they work, how they relate, how they have come to be a particular shape or so complex. Other paths are more interested in, and more suited for, the discovery of 'why?' Why do we exist at all? Why are we here? Why do we suffer? Why can our relationships prove so ecstatic and so destructive?

This is not the place and I am not the right person to attempt an analysis of the human condition from the scientific perspective – that is, human beings seen as a complex matrix of electro-chemical, biological components in which the relationship between nurture and nature is both complicated and unresolved. My intention is much more limited: to see if, in the light of what we have said about God, there are things about being human that lead us to view growing up and maturing in a church school environment as in any way distinctive.

Physical beings

I have read many books and heard it said in frequent conversations that the distinctive Christian understanding of being human is that each individual is made in the image of God. Too often this is asserted as though it is both self-evident and the last word on the subject. At the very most it can only be the first word. It assumes that we first of all know, at least in part, what the nature of the God is in whose image we are made. Hence the last chapter. But it also requires an immediate disclaimer. We are, among other things, physical beings. Whatever else being made in God's image means it does not mean that, because we are physical, God is a physical being, only in a special God kind of way. The Hebrew people were very clear that God was not like the gods of the neighbouring peoples whom they saw in temples and paraded round their streets – images of wood and stone (see Isaiah 44:9-20). The prophets scorned those who bowed to idols, for unlike the God of heaven such gods achieved nothing. There was a clear commandment that the people should not make or worship images of God as though he were an idol like other gods. Nor was the relationship with God to be understood in the physical way that worshippers of the Baals understood it, which led to their use of temple prostitutes. As Jesus states in John's Gospel: 'God is Spirit, and those who worship him must worship in spirit and truth' (John 4:24).

One of the reasons why the name of God in the Old Testament was neither written in full nor spoken was in part because using a person's name was understood to give the user power over the other. But it was also because God is such a mystery that even his name does not encapsulate all he is. Nevertheless, it was to be revered – treated with reverence. One danger of our calling God Father, as Jesus taught us to, is that by its very nature the word links into our physicality. This is why the Lord's Prayer starts with 'Our Father' but immediately qualifies it with 'who art in heaven' – or in the more modern version 'Our Father in heaven'. We are being reminded that while Father says something very important about God we have to understand that in a special way. It also says something very important about us – if God is Father, he is Father of all people and that makes all humanity a single family. Amidst all that seems so ready to divide us – race, culture, colour, religion, national identity – the reality, for the Christian, is that the Fatherhood of God unites us. Although

Christian history sometimes gives the lie to it, the Christian faith has an inclusive understanding of our humanity.

Church schools should not just proclaim the Christian understanding of inclusiveness but live it out as communities of inclusion.

Our physical nature, then, is to be seen as a gift of God within the order of creation and is therefore precious. But in itself it does not imply that God is physical, subject to the same constraints of time and space as we are. Our physical being is important – it is one of the most significant means by which we express ourselves, undertake action, are recognised. The Hebrew way of understanding this was rather different from that of the Greeks. The Greek view, which has tended to dominate Western thinking, sees the human person as a 'body-encased spirit'. Some views would go further and say that the spirit is 'entrapped' in a body. The body is viewed as of dubious value and something to be 'shuffled off'. The Hebrew view is that we are 'inspirited bodies' – the Genesis myth says we are dust that God has breathed into. But the dust, the body, is important; not a prison for the spirit but the Spirit's temple, as St Paul said. It is also why Paul talks about us having a new kind of body in the resurrection life God has in store for us. We do not – whatever Christian piety has sometimes suggested – become disembodied. We are 'embodied' but with a new kind of body. At one level, of course, this is a kind of inspired speculation, but at another it reminds us that, for the Christian, the body, our physical being, is very important. We should take care of it, not abuse it. Healthy eating is not just a modern fad; it is a reflection of this Christian understanding of our nature.

Sex

While we are about it, we should consider the implications this has concerning sex. The power of sex gives it its wonder and its danger. So much emphasis has been given in certain strands of Christian teaching to the dangers of the sexual drive – its ability to motivate abuse, break relationships, feed destructive fantasy and lust – that it can feel as though Christians think all sexual activity is basically wrong and is only allowed by God's indulgence. That is a travesty of what Christians should be teaching. Sex is part of what it is to be human, a gift of God, a good thing to be delighted in and enjoyed but within a proper responsibility and discipline. Sex is not simply a physical matter. The vital context for sex is the nature of the relationship in which it expresses itself. That is why sex education in schools should never be just a matter of the biological/physical mechanics, the techniques of reproduction and contraception. These may be important in themselves but they are not enough. Sex education must be grounded in a proper understanding of appropriate relationships and a discipline (a morality) about sex. Current sexual morality is certainly very different from that of a century ago. Part of the discussion in Christian circles is whether sexual morals are absolute or are themselves subject to development and context.

To be willing to discuss issues of sexual relationships and sexual responsibility in relation to the Christian viewpoint is something a church school should be promoting, without preaching or being judgemental.

Relationships

The above brings us to one of the most important things that can be said about our humanity as beings made in the image of God:

we are made for relationship. This reflects the Trinity relationship that is at the very heart of the nature of God and therefore of what it is to be human. Numerous studies have been carried out over the years, and hundreds of books written on the subject of children's development in terms of their relationships – primarily with their mother but also with their father and siblings and others, as well as with their community of origin. Relationships are formative in children's development: in their maturing, their personal growth and, of course, their social skills.

It doesn't take academic studies to tell us that good relationships from an early age are beneficial, and inadequate early relationships can be damaging for life. It is 'common' sense. But different cultures and different ages would describe 'good relations' in different ways. Stereotypically, the Victorian father was a distant authority figure who believed that children should be seen and not heard. Emotional involvement and display between father and child was thought to be unmanly on the one hand and inappropriate for the child on the other. How many young people from such a background grew up with a picture of God as austere and distant, remote from the inner emotional turmoil of youth, judgemental and harsh on discipline? The experience of earthly fathers shapes the way the heavenly Father is viewed – God made in the image of man! I once met a lad who found the Lord's Prayer very difficult to say because of his dad. The boy had come home from school one afternoon to find the body of his mother chopped to pieces in the bath. His father had done it.

It is not just fathers who can influence how we see God. The relationship of any authority figure, including teachers, can make its mark. It is why relationships in the learning community are so important, not least those between students and teachers.

It is important to give specific relationships their significant place but not to misrepresent their influence. While it is true that, for example, a very traumatic early relationship involving abuse can scar a person for life, it is the whole range of our relationships that builds up our understanding of other people and helps develop our self-image. So our understanding of God is shaped not only by how we have viewed our fathers or mothers – there will be many other relationships that have an influence.

But what are the aspects of relationships that a Christian seeks to emphasise and which a church school should encourage?

Worth

Our relationships are what give us worth – or not. When we say that being made in God's image means each and every individual has infinite worth, worth to God, we are acknowledging the supreme importance each of us attaches to having worth. The invitation to develop a relationship with God holds the promise that in this relationship, if in no other, we are valued, our worth assured. Having a deep sense of worth is vital to our well-being, our wholeness, our self-image.

Christian teaching has tended to emphasise pride as the source of our moral and spiritual dis-ease. It comes from the Genesis story of Adam and Eve's disobedience and, of course, pride can be a very real problem – especially the human pride that puts itself in the place of God. But experience, not least experience of children and young people, leads me to believe that the most damaging thing to the human spirit is not pride but a lack of proper self-worth. It is damaging of the self and damaging of relationships with others.

A school community has no higher task than to help children and young people develop a deep and proper sense of their worth.

What is distinctive about a church school in this respect is how it understands what constitutes that worth. And for the Christian it can be shaped by nothing less than the story and person of Jesus. St Paul talks about growing up into maturity, the full stature of Christ. The mark of the mature person is, says Paul, to be gauged by what we learn from Jesus about what it is to be human.

Possessions

It might be assumed that we all have the same idea about what it is to be human and that Jesus has nothing distinctive to say. But on reflection we quickly see that this is not the case. For example, in the minds of many the most telling aspect of being human is that we are consumers. Current Western culture is dominated by consumerism and the economic model that goes with it. It makes it all too easy for our worth to be seen in terms of either our economic productivity or the 'stuff' that we acquire. The Western capitalist system encourages and needs us to be acquisitive, hungry for ever more things. The financial crisis of 2008 and the years following has meant a tightening of belts alongside debates about how far we can spend ourselves out of the mess. But it seems we are still wedded to the notion that our happiness, our sense of well-being, our worth, can chiefly be discovered in the things with which we surround ourselves. This, of course, is actually a fantasy. We have been fed lies by image-makers and advertisements to fool us into thinking this way. We know, and surveys back it up, that happiness and worth are not brought by the things we pick off the shelves or buy from catalogues or online. But we are not totally convinced, and credit bills show to what lengths we are willing to go, even in difficult times, to find happiness through purchasing yet more possessions. Happiness and worth, of course, are not the same thing. Confusing them has been one of the failures of modern Western civilisation.

The fantasy is fed by both anxiety about whether we really do have worth in ourselves and the competitive individualism that keeps us looking over our shoulder to see what others have. Fear and envy are powerful drivers. The Christian faith seeks to help us to dispel our fear and overcome our envy. The most frequently used phrase in the Bible is 'Do not be afraid' or 'Fear not.' The promise is that, if we could only love and know ourselves to be loved, fear would be lessened. To paraphrase 1 John 4:18a: 'Perfect love casts out, dispels fear.' So, we might add, does a proper sense of worth.

Jesus had a number of things to say about possessions, his words seeming to advocate a kind of austerity. He instructed his disciples not to take extra sets of clothing when going off on a preaching mission, and he said we should not be anxious about food and clothes. He himself appears to have lived very simply.

In some Christian teaching this has led to a condemnation of those who create and acquire wealth. Clearly there are inappropriate and indeed illegal ways of doing both, but the distinctive aspect of Jesus' teaching goes much deeper. What is ultimately important is not what we possess, be that great or small, but our attitudes to possessions, both those we have and those we would like to have. It is when possessions, 'stuff', become our main concern, our aim, our ambition, that there is trouble. It is then that, in Jesus' view, they take on the character of an idol. They become our ultimate concern, our god. That is why greed, or avarice, is seen by Paul, for example, as being linked to idolatry. What matters is where your heart is, and for Jesus that should be set on God and the things of God which enhance the human spirit, not on material possessions – good as they may be in themselves. It is this 'simplicity' of spirit that is called for, rather than the complexity of having and getting.

Within that simplicity there was for Jesus also a strong sense of gratitude – of thanksgiving for what we do have. Underlying and pervading this attitude are two key points. First, we should not allow ourselves to be dominated by possessions – they should not become our top priority (our god) because that is a form of idolatry. Second, we should be generous with what we have, because God is generous, which is why Jesus suggested that if we have two coats, we should give one to the person who has none.

A church school should be a place where attitudes towards possessions and the values of generosity and gratitude are discussed, explored and encouraged. To this extent, a church school may well be counter-cultural.

Even the youngest children these days seem to have the latest electronic equipment: iPods, mobile phones, whatever. As any parent knows, it is not easy to limit a youngster's desire to have what their friends have. But that should not preclude it from being a topic for discussion and challenge. An alternative to the notion that what is most important is 'consumer woman' or 'economic man' is the idea that we are made for 'worship' (worth-ship) – to acknowledge God's worth and to discover in that something of our own.

Love

If God is love, as was asserted in the last chapter, then to be made in the image of God must mean that love should be central to what it is to be human. But, as we noted before, love can be a slippery term with a number of nuances of meaning. The story of Jesus, his life, death and resurrection, is fundamental in shaping the Christian understanding of what love means at both its most particular and its most universal. The love human beings are to have at the heart of their being and to live by in all aspects of their lives is a self-giving, sacrificial love – a love we experience more fully by 'giving it away'. In the words of a children's song from some decades ago: 'Love is like a magic penny – the more you give it away the more you have.'

Because love is not coercion or manipulation (although it might be used as the excuse for either) it is always risky – risking the pain of its rejection. But this risk is central and informs much of Christian spirituality. It means that at the heart of the Christian understanding of what it is to be human, self is precious but is never the first priority. This creates a direct conflict with what in many ways shapes our human creatureliness – in our natural inheritance (the selfish gene), in our psychological make-up (the ego), in much moral failure (self-centredness). And here is a key distinction: while the self (each individual internally and in relation to others) is of high significance (Jesus called us to love ourselves), self-centredness is a dangerous and often destructive distortion. It gets our relationships wrong – with our true selves, with others, with God.

In the formative years of infancy and subsequent identity-confusion associated with puberty, the place of the self is important. The ego has to develop to be healthy. But to get fixated on the self, as if that is all that really matters, is to be both infantile and adolescent, not a fully mature human being.

Part of a school's task is to help infants and adolescents on their journey to maturity. To grow in a self-giving love is to be on that journey in the presence and with the guidance of Jesus and his Spirit.

Success and failure

I have always been suspicious of that form of Christianity which says that if you succeed it is all the work of God and if you fail it is all down to you. There is, of course, truth in the idea that all things come from God and it is of his own that we give him. But God also gave us abilities and gifts, and perseverance and courage to develop them. We have our part to play in the way we use what we are given and what we are. And when that is creative and works well we should celebrate that – whether it be academic success, sporting achievement, artistic expression, acts of kindness, overcoming adversity, or being a good colleague. Human beings do succeed and there should be nothing half-hearted in our celebration of that success. The important thing, however, is not to define success too narrowly. This is one of the problems with the current drive to assess educational achievement only through SATs, GCSEs, and so forth. It is the problem with success defined by what is done and not by what one is. A faith that focuses on a man whose life ended in execution has its own distinctive view of what constitutes ultimate success.

But if success is important to being human then it is equally important to understand what to do about failure. And we all fail – at some time, at some point. The notion that there is no such thing as failure, only deferred success, is a dangerous one. It refuses to be true to the reality of what it is to be human. Having failed is not at all the same thing as being a failure. To treat someone as a failure – i.e. to write them off, devalue them, consider them as having no worth – is to dehumanise them. To acknowledge that there has been failure is to be true to the situation, which then has to be dealt with. At the heart of the Christian gospel is the belief that God, the loving Father, is a forgiving God, offering a forgiveness that is transforming. The death of Jesus shows the cost of such forgiveness to God. His resurrection reveals that the forgiveness he offered, even while being crucified, is vindicated, goes beyond death. To be forgiving is the way God is, the way he wants us to be. This loving forgiveness helps us to be free of the fear of failure and to be willing to risk exciting new things – even if we might fail.

In the Lord's Prayer we ask that we might be forgiven as we forgive others. The implication is not that God doesn't forgive us if we ourselves are not forgiving. Rather it is to do with the fact that in our understanding of failure we both acknowledge our own need to be forgiven and also exercise that gracious loving act of offering forgiveness to others. If we fail to feel 'in our souls' the importance of restoring our relationship with others through forgiveness, we shall fail to see the need for the restoration of our relationship with God by responding to his forgiveness, and hence we will block, as it were, God's forgiveness of us. At its deepest level such forgiveness is not only for 'sins', wrong actions; it is for 'sin' itself – that brokenness of relationship which is at the heart of the human predicament. And forgiveness deals not only with the fact of fault or failure, but also with the guilt that accompanies failure and that can be so corrosive to the human spirit.

From a belief in the gospel of forgiveness, revealed and enacted by Jesus, a church school should have a creative and vibrant approach to failure and to those inappropriate expectations that so often fuel a sense of failure. To fail is not a disaster. It provides a critical opportunity for learning and for transformation.

Partners

There is a great deal of discussion in education these days about the way in which schools can form partnerships – with other schools and academic institutions, with service providers, with business and industry. Partnership is an essential aspect of living in society, and the story of the creation of Eve in the book of Genesis reflects the sense that it is 'not good' for human beings to be on their own. They need both companions and colleagues.

For the Christian this is grounded not just in the fact that we are social creatures, or in the Genesis account of God at the start of creation creating woman (Eve) as a companion for man (Adam). It is rooted, rather, in the fact that God calls us to be his companions (to walk with him) and colleagues (joint workers with him). Human beings are not simply creatures. They are sharers in the process of sustaining and stewarding creation, in the process of drawing humanity into a fully responsive and responsible relationship with God, with one another and with the world and in bringing in the kingdom (the rule) of justice, compassion, love and mercy. The Christian understanding sees human beings not simply as creatures who are 'done to' by God but as co-workers with God. This is a position of privilege and responsibility.

This has implications for the way we view the world and our role in its stewardship rather than exploitation, and more will be said about that in a later chapter. But it also has implications for the way we view each other – as fellow workers, as companions on a journey.

In church schools, all members of the learning community should be given the opportunity to make their contribution, and the part each can play should be strongly respected. Children are clearly not there 'to be done to' – they are active partners in their learning.

FOUR

A matter of belief – the Church

No man is an island,
Entire of itself.
Each is a piece of the continent,
A part of the main.

(John Donne)

For just as the body is one and has many members, and all the members of the body, though many, are one body, so it is with Christ . . . the body does not consist of one member but of many.

(St Paul, 1 Corinthians 12:12, 14)

Nature, it might be said, has little interest in the individual. What matters is the survival of the species. The abundance of seeds that a dandelion produces is its insurance policy to help ensure that, however adverse the conditions, at least a few will survive to grow into mature plants. That individual seeds will perish is the acceptable cost.

But what might be true of seed heads feels a harsh, uncaring pragmatism when it comes to human beings. It's true that on the battlefield, decisions sometimes have to made involving a cost in casualties, and at worst that calculation can appear callous, as though individuals are expendable for the sake of military success, put down as collateral damage. In calmer times, however, and on more moral consideration, individuals are understood to have worth in themselves rather than being merely means to ends. Indeed, it is one of the basic moral tenets that people should be seen and treated as ends in themselves and not as means to an end.

This is not an explicit or distinctive Christian moral imperative but it reflects the infinite worth that is put on an individual in the Christian ethic. The hairs of our head are counted; the God who cares for the birds of the air has an individual concern for each human being, who he considers of yet more worth (Luke 12:7). Protestant theology emphasises the faith of the individual believer and their relationship with God through Christ. It can be seen as a very individualistic faith, with the focus on an individual's salvation. By contrast the Roman Catholic tradition has tended to emphasise the role of the Church through whose sacraments the believer gains salvation. It is, as it were, the species that matters more than the individual.

The individual and the corporate

The Scriptures hold the individual and the corporate in a nice balance. In St Paul's image of the body, each member, each organ of the body, has its value and has the right to respect, reverence even, no matter how lowly it might appear to be. Each has its appropriate function and makes its contribution to the whole. Differentiation is both necessary and valued. The body is made up of its constituent parts, which, together, comprise the Body of Christ. The individual parts have their place but their significance, in this model, is found in the role they fulfil within the whole body. What really matters is not so much what gifts each individual can display, although they are important as the work of the Spirit, but the way those gifts are used for the building up of the Church.

Baptism

The way in which the individual and the corporate relate is demonstrated in the different understandings and theologies that churches have produced with regard to baptism. The tradition of the Middle Ages was to require a baby to be baptised within a short time of birth, because through the sacrament of Baptism the infant was incorporated into the Body of Christ, the Church, and salvation assured. To die as an infant without having been baptised put that infant's immortal soul in peril. The emphasis was on what the body of believers, the Church, did through a priest in the name of the Triune God. The infant's individual faith was not the issue. It was, as it were, the faith of the Church and God's grace that ensured the salvation of the child.

With its emphasis upon individual faith the Reformation switched attention to the significance of a personal expression of faith, albeit by parents and godparents on behalf of an infant. The need for an expression of personal faith as a prerequisite for baptism led to the creation of denominations such as Baptists, who decline to baptise infants and reserve baptism for adult believers. The Church of England has retained infant baptism as the norm but increasingly seeks to incorporate this within a main act of worship in which the whole congregation is present. Among other things, it is seeking to show through this that there is a relationship between an individual's worth and faith and their place within the whole people of God, the Church.

This theological point might well appear arcane and hardly of relevance to what goes on in a school. But that is not the case. A school should certainly have values that express its concern for the individual, but it is also a community, and the way individuals relate to and play their part in that community is also highly significant. Indeed, it is part of a young person's social development. The school, in other words, is not, and cannot be, simply a collection of individuals, each having absolute rights regardless of others. Rather, it is a community where the contribution of each to the life of the whole is valued, where the needs of the many also have to be considered, and where no one has either exclusive or no rights. To this extent there should, of course, be both sharing and mutual caring, one for another.

What the church school is seeking to do is to ground the relationship between the individual and the whole community in its understanding of the Christian view of what it means to be a human being in community, a believer in a church community.

Exclusion

A practical example may illustrate this. The head teacher of a church comprehensive school in a parish in inner Birmingham came to the reluctant conclusion that he had to exclude a pupil. When he told me what he had done he said: 'I know you'll remind me about the parable of the shepherd who went off after the one lost sheep, leaving the 99 to fend for themselves. But I have to worry about the 99 sheep as well, and on this occasion their well-being is being undermined by the one lost sheep.' It is a dilemma every head teacher has to face from time to time. There is no easy resolution and the Christian does not have a quick answer in the back of the book – not even the back of the Bible.

Some church schools have a clear policy that they will never exclude a pupil. Others feel with equal conviction that it is not possible to make such an absolute commitment. But a church school, and not least its foundation governors, would want to ask some serious questions if there were a constant stream of exclusions – not only about the individual miscreants but about the whole ethos of the school community, its behaviour policy, even the way in which its curriculum was engaging with young people.

The household

Various images are used for the Church: e.g. Body, Bride, Congregation, the new Israel. Each has its scriptural basis and its own particular emphasis. But perhaps most commonly the Church is described as a family, characterised by that close relationship of affection and commitment found in families at their best. Sadly there are also occasions when the Church resembles a family at its worst – squabbling, self-obsessed, split by controversy and even, on occasions, violence. The family image obviously has both its strengths and its weaknesses. The emotional ties can be for good or bad. A less often-used image but one that is also found in Scripture is the household. When St Paul and Silas were in prison (Acts 16:23-29) the jailer was horror-struck after a violent earthquake to discover that all the doors had come open, and he would have killed himself had not Paul stopped him, explaining that all the prisoners were still in their cells. The jailer then asked what he should do to be saved (v. 30). Paul and Silas told him: 'Believe on the Lord Jesus, and you will be saved, you and your household' (Acts 16:31).

'Household' does not resonate with quite the same warmth of intimate relationship as 'family' and can suggest an outdated social divide of upstairs and downstairs. It also comes from a culture and period rather different from that of the modern Western nuclear or fractured family. On the other hand, it speaks of a more inclusive, flexible form of community in which all sorts and conditions of people have their place, not least the stranger and the alien.

The church school might wish to explore the images of 'family' and 'household' and discover what these might say for its learning community.

The established church

We have already noted that in talking about a church school there are some marked differences between a Church of England and a Roman Catholic church school. This reflects what each church has historically come to see as the purpose of its investment in education. And this in turn arises from the role each church plays, or sees itself as playing, within society. So how does the Church of England understand its role?

The name is obviously a big clue. The Anglican Church in England is the national church, established in law. It is not only 'in England' but 'of England'. Being the established church has a number of ramifications such as the fact that its laws or measures are not simply rules set out for itself, by itself, but are enacted by Parliament. They become part of the law of the land. Bishops are appointed by the monarch on the recommendation of the Church and the Prime Minister. These things are not true of – for example – the Baptist or Roman Catholic Church, at least not at the moment.

Equally, the Church of England is involved in certain aspects of the state in a way other churches are not. For example, the monarch is crowned by the Archbishop of Canterbury, and among the monarch's titles is Defender of the Faith, Head of the Church of England. The chaplain to the House of Commons is a priest of the Church of England. A number of bishops have the right to sit in the House of Lords. National events, such as the thanksgiving service after the Falklands war or the funeral of Princess Diana, take place in an Anglican church or cathedral. At a more local level, it is the Anglican parish church that is normally viewed as the 'civic' church.

Ever since the Reformation, law and common custom have given the Church of England a unique place in the life of the nation. Whether this will remain so is not entirely certain as there are voices within and outside the Church calling for its disestablishment.

The Church of England can boast of the fact that through its parish system it has a presence and sense of responsibility for every square inch of the country and all its inhabitants. Clearly that does not mean that everyone sees themselves either as a member of the Church of England or even as Christian. In a multi-cultural, multi-faith society that is plainly not the case, although it is interesting to see how high a percentage of people do still put themselves down as both Christian and Church of England when it comes to census forms. What the boast actually reflects is the Church's self-understanding in its pastoral role as being there not just for members of its congregations but for everyone. Anyone, whether they be Church of England or not, Christian or not, of faith or not, can call upon a Church of England priest for pastoral care. Similarly, in its works of social justice, the Church displays its concern for the well-being of the community at large rather than simply its members. It seeks to live out what has been described as God's bias to the poor and the vulnerable, no matter what their race, religion, culture or colour may be.

Implications for admissions

This has significant implications for the Church of England's approach to its schools, which are there for the whole community, not just the local congregation. And this is, or should be, reflected in their admission policies. Those church schools that have exclusive admission policies, within the constraints of the national guidelines, are not reflecting the Church of England's own self-understanding as a Church.

It might be argued that, in an urban situation, where parents have a choice of school for their children, a more exclusive policy by a church school is both understandable and makes a statement about the distinctive religious nature of a church school. Personally, I do not think this holds water. In a rural setting, where the only local school is a church school, there must be an open admissions policy – the school, like the church, is there for the whole community, not just for members of the church. Nor is it the role of the Church of England to create elitist schools through their admission policies. Many church schools with an open admissions policy are good or outstanding and very popular with parents. That is how it should be. Church schools should be concerned that the good reputation they have is not derived from a quasi selection process that seeks to ensure only the 'best' children enter the school. Of all schools, a church school should have a broader vision of its role than its place in the league table.

A Church of England school should reflect the place the Church has in the life of the nation as the established church and its pastoral availability to every member of the community. This should be reflected in a school's admission policy. Foundation governors, especially in a voluntary aided school where the governors are the admissions authority, should ensure that its policy is true to this distinctive feature of the Church of England.

Liturgy

One of the traditional treasures of the Church of England, alongside the King James Bible, is the Book of Common Prayer. While there are many who still value the beautiful cadencies of its language and the rhythm of its liturgy, the Church itself has spent considerable effort in producing a more modern style of worship. But it has done so still believing in the value of Common Prayer; that is, of worship common to all of its parishes. While provision is made for variety and local choice in the many resources now available within the books of *Common Worship* (2000), nevertheless the forms of service are still determined by the Church at large through its General Synod. They are not simply the product of the local worship group or minister.

Of course this could be seen as part of the Church's mechanism for control, and there is some truth in this. It is its liturgy that has traditionally most clearly expressed the faith of the Church of England, while other churches have depended on Confessions, Encyclicals or hymns. There is therefore good reason why it has sought to ensure the 'orthodoxy' of what worship expresses while at the same time allowing for creativity and local expression. This 'orthodoxy' has meant, more so in the past, that members of the Church of England are able to recognise its forms of worship, feeling at home with the familiar, no matter which parish church they attend.

In this common liturgical provision the Church draws upon the traditions developed over the centuries in devising the shape of its worship. These traditions ensure a certain 'quality' of worship, grounded in an understanding of the corporate nature of congregational worship, a form of worship that is quite different from individual personal prayer. It is this sense of liturgical 'shape', together with an awareness of the liturgical seasons of the Church's year, that is reflected in the advice on collective worship offered to schools. The nature of that shape and how it can influence school worship is dealt with more fully in chapter 10.

The liturgical tradition of the Church of England can help enrich school collective worship in a distinctive way.

A broad church

The Church of England has traditionally viewed itself as both Catholic and Reformed. That is, it has its roots within the pre-Reformation

Church and believes itself to be part of the universal/catholic Church while also holding to the insights of the Protestant reformers with their emphasis on the authority of Scripture and independence from the rule of Rome. This via media position grew out of the historical situation that saw the Church of England come into existence, namely Henry VIII's split with Rome over the matter of his divorce from Catherine of Aragon (and his desire to appropriate the wealth of the monasteries). For its critics this has produced a church that is too inclusive, too broad, too vague on what it believes, struggling in times of controversy (such as now) to keep its catholic, traditionalist, evangelical and liberal wings in communion with one another. For others again, however, this 'broad church' characteristic is exactly what appeals to them about the Church of England. It appears less dogmatic, less authoritarian than some other churches or denominations, without rigid boundaries of membership or doctrine.

For good or ill, this is how the Church of England is, and it is reflected in the distinctive nature of its schools insofar as they are open and inclusive. This can make some of them look no different from community schools. At best, they have a distinctive openness combined with a lively faith, which is creative and life enhancing.

Reasonable

The authority of a church is derived from a complex combination of various factors. These include: the Scriptures, tradition, credal statements, its ordained ministry, charismatic leadership. An individual might add to this list: personal experience and the voice of conscience. Different churches and individuals place different emphasis upon each of these. To put it crudely, a conservative evangelical is likely to place strongest emphasis upon Scripture and be less concerned about tradition. A more Catholic position would emphasise tradition and the statements of the Pope. An independent church is more likely to appeal to charismatic leadership and the faith experience of its members.

The Church of England has attempted, with varying degrees of success, to hold a number of these together – seeing them as strands in a rope giving strength and durability. At one level this can be seen in what is called the Lambeth Quadrilateral, a statement which, in 1888, set out the four things Anglicans felt essential to their existence as a church and central in any conversations about unity with other churches. These were: the Scriptures, the Creeds (Apostles' and Nicene), the two sacraments of Baptism and Holy Communion, and the historic ministry of bishops.

A different set of characteristics has brought Scripture, tradition, reason and experience together. And reason is of particular significance when it comes to schools and education. It is linked with what was said in chapter 2 concerning God and truth. While, of course, faith is a personal stance involving commitment to something that cannot be proved in the objective way of science, it is not simply dependent on irrational beliefs or subjective feelings. It has a language and a discipline about its discourse that puts limits upon what is believed by those wishing to be considered members of the Church. Although faith and theology cannot be totally confined to rational logic it is not thereby forced to be irrational. To use a rather ugly word, it might be called para-rational, indicating it is reasonable but goes beyond reason. In more down-to-earth language, faith has its reasons – but they are reasons of the heart as well as of the head.

Even so, the head is important within the Church of England's understanding. Inner faith experience has its part to play in the Christian journey, but reason and careful thought are also important. The search for God's truth, the truth about all there is, encourages the Christian to explore understanding from wherever it comes. While there have been famous (and even infamous) occasions when the Christian Church has opposed and obstructed the search for scientific explanation when it has felt its faith position to be threatened (e.g. by Galileo or Darwin), it has also been instrumental in extending the boundaries of knowledge. A world that is believed to have been made by God is a world of wonder to explore and understand – not to view with either suspicion or superstition.

Church schools should be places of delight in the discovery of knowledge – places where boundaries of understanding are ever expanding and the implications of our knowledge are also examined.

The use of reason is not only a matter of exploring the world of knowledge presented by scientists, artists and engineers. Its value is also shown in the Church's willingness to put its own faith, tradition and Scriptures to a critical examination. As far as the Scriptures are concerned, this is, in any sustained way, a fairly modern phenomenon; one that developed from the nineteenth century onwards with a whole range of critical approaches examining how we might best understand the Bible in other than a literalist way. So biblical studies today will, among other things, look at the historical, cultural setting for a passage of Scripture; ask what kind of writing it is (e.g. poetry, myth, history, legend, letter, hymn, etc.); consider the author's intention at the time of writing and how it is understood now; explore whether the passage is from a single author or the result of a long oral tradition, whether it is a statement of historical accuracy or shaped by the desire to convey a position of faith. For some people, such studies have made them feel as though their faith is being undermined. For others, it has been invigorating and faith enhancing, opening up vistas of new understanding and placing faith more securely in the public arena rather than in a closed ecclesiastical box.

The examination of the text of Scripture has largely been in the hands of critical scholars. They have looked at how the text came to be written and what oral traditions it relied on. They have considered the ways in which the text developed and how it answered questions posed by changing circumstances. The Gospels, for example, have been probed to see what sayings could be traced to the actual words of Jesus and which were the product of the early church. But there is also a strand of critique that arises not from an examination of the text itself so much as an examination of the relationship of what is said in the text concerning the demands of love or compassion or justice. In other words, if a passage of Scripture leads an individual or a church or society to perpetrate injustice, to fail to be compassionate or loving, then the authority of the text itself or the way it has been traditionally interpreted has to be questioned. This willingness of a faith to critique itself and its sources of authority is, it seems to me, essential for any faith or church that seeks to be creative and vigorous.

Far from church schools attempting to 'brainwash' children about faith, they should encourage the exploration of what faith is and what it is about, bringing to it the critical tools of reason as well as the wonder of belief.

Tradition

The appeal of the Church to tradition speaks of the significance the Church gives to those who have gone before those currently in membership and to the wisdom that has grown over the years. At worst this can merely mean the dead hand of a backward-looking conservatism that assumes the only good things are in and from the past. More positively, tradition prevents the domination of the new and the novel; the belief that everything that has gone before is encrusted in an irrelevant antiquity. In a time of rapid and constant change it is important that individuals and organisations have a sense of rootedness in something that is not swept chaotically along on the tide of novelty, whether that be a rootedness of place, of culture, or of faith. This has the value of giving a sense of belonging to what is not ephemeral. Christianity has this sense of belonging and the Church of England treasures it.

Church schools have the advantage not only of being part of a corporate school history that stretches back for two hundred years but also of sharing in an ethos that draws upon two thousand years of story, reflection, wisdom and experience.

This in itself is a learning resource, as children are helped to develop skills of historical awareness, of reflecting on the influence of context, time and place in the values people hold, modify and develop. A school community will have its own traditions, both explicit and implicit, that can be usefully explored and that enrich the life of the community. The ability to critique and develop such traditions and not simply accept and blindly follow them is also important.

Experience

If tradition speaks specifically to a corporate perspective, experience is more to do with the individual. The authority of tradition can dominate from beyond oneself and give very little place for the individual conscience or life-story. The two strands need to be held together, and experience honours the value of the individual that the Christian ethos sets such store by. The Church has been strengthened and invigorated by the spiritual and life experience of individuals, some of whom have not initially been particularly acceptable to the church establishment yet have deepened and renewed the Church's tradition and spiritual life. One has only to think of a St Francis or a Julian of Norwich in the past, or a John Wesley (who remained an Anglican all his life) and John Robinson in more modern times.

There is currently considerable emphasis upon the role and responsibility of pupils and students in their own learning. Their learning experience is not simply a matter to be tested and assessed by others but something for the pupils themselves to reflect upon, value and evaluate. By doing so, that experience itself is critiqued and deepened. It is no longer a matter of 'How well do you think I am doing?' but rather one of 'How well do I think I am doing?' 'Where are the improvements, where are the weaknesses?' 'What will take me to the next step?'

Not all experience is so directly associated with formal learning in the school setting, although, of course, all experiences can be a source of learning. The life experience of students and pupils is a rich source of their learning, and schools that aim to take each individual seriously will draw upon that varied and individual experience, not only for the development of the individuals themselves but as part of the enrichment of other pupils and students. There is much in young people's experience to be celebrated.

Unfortunately, not all of life's experiences are either pleasant or positive. Every teacher who is alert to the well-being and individuality of their students will be conscious of the influence of experiences beyond the classroom and the school environment. Homes can be places of stress as well as comfort, of trauma as well as support, and such experiences will inevitably have a telling impact upon young people. No school that claims a caring ethos with a respect for each and every member can do less than take such experiences seriously. Doing so is, at the very least, part of the general pastoral care of pupils, and in extreme cases involves a school in the sensitive and potentially distressing process of safeguarding, defined by the government as: 'The process of protecting children from abuse or neglect, preventing impairment of their health and development, and ensuring they are growing up in circumstances consistent with the provision of safe and effective care that enables children to have optimum life chances and enter adulthood successfully.' The Christian story places a strong emphasis upon the significance of children and their well-being. One has only to think of Jesus' attitude towards children: 'Unless you change and become like children, you will never enter the kingdom of heaven' (Matthew 18:3b). To hurt, or cause a child to stumble, drew from Jesus particular condemnation (Matthew 18:6; Mark 9:42; Luke 17:2). But there is also in the Christian story much about transformation, compassion and healing. Bad experiences are not trivialised but they are not the end of the story either.

Church schools should above all be places of hope, believing in the possibility of positive outcomes from bad experiences. The cross and resurrection teach that. But such hope is realised both by prayer (an awareness of God's place in the process) and by care (the part to be played by those supporting the youngster).

FIVE

A matter of belief – the world

The world is charged with the grandeur of God.

(Gerard Manley Hopkins)

The poet's bold assertion above has been echoed by artists throughout the ages. Painters, musicians, psalmists have not only found inspiration in the world of nature but have seen there the hand of God, his grandeur and glory as well as his judgement and wrath. Websites from Christian groups (especially in America) reproduce pictures from space and assert that the vastness and beauty of the galaxies prove the hand of God in creation. They do no such thing of course, and over-bloated piety merely plays into the hands of sceptics and secularists. It is faith, not proof, that declares this speck of dust and the vast universe it exists within to be the result of a divine act of creation. And Christianity is not the first (or last) religion to make such a claim.

Nature as it is

It is easy to drift from a powerful sense of wonder into sentimentality and there has been no shortage of artists, musicians and writers who have done just that. It is important that in encouraging children in their sense of wonder and delight in nature a school does not similarly allow a drift into a sugary view of the world that bears little relation to the way it actually is. In proclaiming God's creative act there can be a convenient amnesia about the darker side of nature

– the nature red in tooth and claw that Tennyson wrote of. Natural disasters such as those that in recent years have hit Haiti or Pakistan are part of that same nature that creates the splendour of alpine sunsets or the intricacy of a butterfly's wing. The TV that brings such wonders into our homes brings also into them the tragedies, the disasters of the world at its most brutish.

A good creation?

In trying to see the picture whole, the Christian faith has to square its belief in a good and loving creator God with the way the world is. The opening stories in Genesis picture creation as a series of events at whose conclusion God not only rests but declares himself pleased with the result. God 'saw everything that he had made, and indeed, it was very good' (Genesis 1:31a). It has been assumed that in making this statement, the writer viewed creation in its origins as being perfect. The same has been assumed of humankind. How could God make something less than perfect? But everyday experience shows that this is not the way things actually are. Chapter 3 of Genesis sets out the Hebrew understanding of what went wrong. It was all down to man's (and woman's) thinking they knew better than God. Human wrong, sin, was seen as the root cause of creation's imperfections, and it has infected the whole universe ever since.

Genesis offers a powerful picture not only of the responsibility we have for what happens to our own species but also of the impact we have upon the wider creation. It is a spiritual not a scientific explanation of the fact that human lives, the world of nature and the universe are less than perfect, if by that we mean that they cause humanity grief. Some would see this as merely yet another example of the hubris in the human psyche which places humankind at the focus of everything that happens. If a volcano erupts in the middle of a wilderness it is a thing of majestic, awesome power and beauty capable of bringing fertility to a barren scene. An eruption near a centre of population is seen as an evil disaster. The human reference colours the description and has implications for what we believe. The one demonstrates the grandeur of the creator God, the other calls into question how good his creation really is.

Fit for purpose

The biblical phrase 'And God saw that it was good' (Genesis 1:10b, 12b, 18b, 21b, 25b, 31a) is capable of an understanding other than simply that here was a perfection in which nothing ever goes wrong. God's declaration could equally have meant 'it is just as I intended it to be'. Or in a more modern phrase – 'it's fit for purpose'. The created order was fit for the purpose God intended for it: to be the setting within which human beings could grow into responsible maturity and respond freely to their loving creator. Such an interpretation is no less anthropocentric than the account of the fall whereby the whole universe went wrong because of Adam and Eve's sin. But it does steer clear of some of the most obvious objections arising from the notion that 'bad' things only happened in the universe after humankind came on the scene. It also retains the understanding that from the outset God knew what he was about and was always 'in control'. The way the world is, is the way God intended it to be. That is small comfort of course to those caught up in tsunamis and devastating floods but it does mean that in the universe as it is a great deal of responsibility is placed upon humankind to respond compassionately in the face of disasters and to learn from them as well.

Global television brings into our homes the constant reminder that nature is amazing but also that this world is a 'vale of tears'. It is no different when it comes to men and women. According to the Psalmist, humankind 'has been made a little lower than the angels and crowned with glory', but to the philosopher Thomas Hobbes the life of man in its natural state is 'solitary, poore, nasty, brutish, and short' (*Leviathan*). There is an ambiguity about creation and the world we live in – at least from our point of view.

There may indeed be an ambiguity about the world of nature but for the Christian the world remains part of a good God's good creation. It is not the creation of either chance or a devil. Although charged with the glory of God it remains God's *creation* – it is not in itself divine. God may be present in all places but the world is not said to be the place of his dwelling in the way the heavens are. As the old hymn 'Alleluia! sing to Jesus' has it: 'Earth your footstall, heaven your throne'. There is, as it were, a distance between God and what he creates – not a distance that results in a lack of care or compassion, but a distance that allows for a proper distinction between the creator and the created. This same distinction has provided humanity with the freedom to investigate the natural order without the inhibitions that would exist were nature understood as being in itself divine or the focus of magic. Such views have certainly been held and stood in the way of the whole scientific enterprise. Today, at a time when some view faith as the enemy of scientific endeavour, it is important to remember that it was people of faith who led much of the advance in scientific knowledge and encouraged disciplined observation and investigation of all aspects of the natural world.

Far from being anti-scientific a church school should be committed to the development of an enthusiastic and rigorous enquiry into the nature of the world around us; one that neither denies the continuing possibility of faith nor shackles science with doctrinaire fundamentalism.

A green school

In the Genesis story Adam was given the responsibility of 'dominion', or 'rule', over all living creatures but there is no indication that he could do just what he liked. It was a responsibility, not a licence for unbridled exploitation. He was placed in the Garden of Eden to care for and work it. We, likewise, are called to be stewards of the resources creation affords. We are neither to worship creation nor to selfishly exploit it.

Ecology has an increasingly significant place in the school curriculum and community life. Early Years children are not only expected to be outside in the open air for a proportion of each day as part of healthy living but are encouraged to engage in the growing of flowers and plants to gain an understanding of the natural environment within which they live and of which they are a part. Many schools now have monitoring systems to show the children the energy use of their school, and transport plans highlight the impact of the car on carbon footprints.

It is good to be green, and in a school where the world is understood to be part of God's good creation the governors have a responsibility to consider just how green their school is or could be.

More than
Caring and
Sharing

SIX

Kingdom values

It may have been the way I was taught but for me the word 'kingdom' always had connotations of place. It was a territory or a country where there was a king. Kingdom does, of course, have that meaning. But when it comes to the opening phrases of the Lord's Prayer, that led to confusion. I wasn't quite sure what it meant when we prayed for God's kingdom to come. Was it a matter of adding to the sum of those countries where people were Christians?

Hopefully, childhood literalism gives way to more sophisticated concepts, but the notion of territory in association with the idea of God's kingdom has not been entirely absent from the spread of Christianity. We used to speak of Christendom, and at times of religious confrontation there is the tendency to slip into this way of thinking as when, for example, people speak of the conflict between the Islamic world and the Christian West.

But the kingdom of God has less to do with geography than with hearts and minds. The kingdom of God is present wherever God's kingly rule is recognised and lived by. Christians may be praying that God's rule will be acknowledged throughout the world, in all places and all countries, but more significantly it is a prayer that God's way for human life, God's purposes for his creation, will prevail in the hearts and minds of all people and over all that he has made. At the personal level this call for God's kingdom to come is a plea that God's rule may come in my heart and in the hearts of all those who join in this prayer. It is a prayer for the coming of that relationship with God in which he is acknowledged as 'king' and with whom I seek to live in loving obedience.

To speak of God's rule could lead to a very legalistic view of what God's kingdom means – a matter of submitting to rules and commandments. The discipline of discipleship does indeed include obedience and there are rules to guide what God requires. Jesus summed it all up in the Golden Rule referred to earlier of 'In everything do to others as you would have them do to you' (Matthew 7:12a). The Church's liturgy sets out the basic law in terms of love of God and love of neighbour. But, like all law, this needs interpretation and elaboration, and needs to develop from what is laid down externally to what is lived by from within. God's rule is more to do with values than with commandments.

So in this chapter we turn from some of the basic Christian beliefs to the values they give rise to and which are embedded in the Christian story. For the main part such values are not unique. They are shared with those of no Christian allegiance but who have been brought up in those places where Christianity has had a long historical influence. They are also shared with other faiths and with those who hold a humanist position. But the emphasis within Christianity is sometimes different and, taken as a whole, such values do create a distinctive ethos that makes sense of them being called 'Christian values'. It is in the foundations for those values, disclosed in the story of the faith and especially in the preaching, teaching and life of Jesus, where the most obvious distinguishing features are to be found. They are often summed up as 'values of the kingdom' or, more simply, 'kingdom values' because they emerge through Jesus' teaching about the kingdom of God, through his kingdom parables and, supremely, through the life, death and resurrection of Jesus, the King.

There is no set or exhaustive list of these values and we shall concentrate here on a just a few of them. The collective worship resource *Values for Life* from Jumping Fish identifies 18 values, whereas the Christian Values for Schools website lists 14. Neither of these includes LOVE but it is clear that this is fundamental to all the other values, so it is with love that we begin.

Love

Christians believe love to be the key to all good relationships – with God, with other people, with creation and with oneself. It is founded in the nature of God's own relationships, both with all he has created and in the relationship within his own being which lies behind what we describe as the Trinity. Love doesn't simply make the world go round; it is the 'driver' of God himself and all his creation.

That is to make a high claim for love and it is not incontrovertible. Some people would argue that power, for example, is more significant both in religion and in human interaction, individually and socially. For all that love is important, it can all too easily be trivialised. Popular use can reduce love to nothing more than a statement of preferred taste. 'I just love coffee but can't stand tea.' It is also open to being abused and degraded. Claims of love can be the basis for emotional blackmail and excuse for sexual abuse.

Although youngsters may well find talk of love 'soppy' or 'uncool', they know deep down that they want love, need love, are desperate for love. The lack of love in their lives can be a major cause not only of unhappiness but of a failure to mature in their own relationships with others.

The association of love with sex makes discussion of the relationship between the two a vital matter so that the two are not simply equated and so that what is distinctive about both is explored and understood.

How does your church school provide opportunities for discussion about the place of love in pupils' lives and, with older students, the relation between love and sex?

The paragraphs above have already indicated that love is not a simple matter. Indeed, it is not obvious exactly how we should describe it. Is it just a matter of the will? After all, Jesus commanded us to love, and obedience to a command involves at least the will. Is it simply an emotion – something we have comparatively little control of? Is it a physical urge to be expressed through sexual activity? Is it just a way of stating a preference of taste? As C. S. Lewis' classic little book *The Four Loves* (1960) shows, the nature of love is diverse. There is, he writes, romantic or erotic love (*eros*), the love of friendship (*philia*), familial love, affection (*storge*) and spiritual love (*agape*).

The notion of love no doubt contains all of these and much more. If it is to be a rich reality in our lives and the lives of others it should relate to the whole of our being – physically, spiritually, emotionally, morally, intellectually, socially. The danger is to reduce that rich range to something more simplistic by an over-emphasis on certain aspects at the expense or even denial of others. This can perhaps be seen most readily in the complex balance of sex and love as part of a responsible relationship. The physical aspect of sex cannot be divorced in a Christian understanding from a loving relationship, which includes the integrity of each person, mutual respect, and commitment. But it is equally dangerous to divorce an understanding of responsible loving relationships from an awareness of the potential power of physical attraction. Similarly, ignoring the spiritual aspect of love is not only to reduce the wonder of its potency in our relationship with the transcendent but can lead to a reductionism that sees human beings merely as a complex network of biochemical interactions.

Of all values, qualities and emotions, true love is the most obviously outgoing. It seeks what is best for the other even at the cost of self. It is the basis for that open valuing of others that should be the mark of every church school. It is the root and the product of worship – for worship at its best both arises from the love of God who is being worshipped and itself deepens the love of the worshipper for God. It is the basis for a delight in and respect for the natural order which develops a sense of responsibility towards the environment, counteracting the selfish exploitation of creation that threatens the sustainability of our planet.

Love, by its nature, is generous and giving.

In what ways might collective worship express the nature of outgoing love both for people and for the environment?

In a verse that many consider to be a summary of the Christian gospel, John tells us that 'God so loved the world that he gave his only Son, so that everyone who believes in him may not perish but may have eternal life' (John 3:16). God expresses his love in this outgoing act of deeply personal and costly generosity, not for his own sake, but for the sake of the world. This is the model for all Christian love. In the first of his letters, John tells us not only that God is love but that he loved us first, and it is because God loved us so much that we should love one another (1 John 4:11). In these verses the Greek word translated as 'love' is agape. It is this form of love that is distinctively understood as Christian love: the love God has for us and which Christians seek, by the grace of God, to emulate. Because God loves all, there is no one who is not loved. In witnessing to this truth about God, Christians are themselves called to show love for all. This is not a matter of liking all. Some people are very difficult to like. Agape love is a matter of attitude, of respect and giving worth, of treating with integrity even when that is costly – all for the sake of the other person, regardless of deserts. This is the foundation of all that is distinctive in a church school. The classical description of what Christianity understands by love is to be found in the so-called 'Hymn to love' in 1 Corinthians 13.

Individuals may have good reason from their own worst experiences to feel they are not loved, and certainly there are too many children who do feel this. But the reality is different, and those who work to convey that reality in church schools will seek to show to their pupils a love that enhances their sense of worth and convinces them they are lovable and loved. Helping others to feel and acknowledge the love within which they are held encourages them to be loving people – outgoing and generous to others even at a cost to themselves.

In looking for what is distinctive about the Christian understanding of the kingdom value of love, we look to the life and teaching of Jesus, himself the King of love. We see it in his attitude towards the sick and the outcast, in his compassion towards the poor, in his willingness to give of himself, and in his ultimate sacrifice. Those who seek to love are making themselves vulnerable – and for young people that is quite a hard lesson to learn. Schools need to consider how they support not only the vulnerable but the vulnerability of those who are otherwise strong.

The nature of love is complex and is much more than a matter of soft or romantic feelings. There is a hard-headed realism required of those who would love. In what ways does a distinctive Christian love inform the policies as well as the vision statement of your church school?

Justice

Justice is the social face of love. It is love in the corporate arena of society and of nations. It is what ensures that the actions of organisations do not disproportionately override, exploit or manipulate the rights and dignity of individuals. Justice is what school governors need to be aware of when acting as a corporate group, managing the institution of the school for the benefit of all without trampling on the worth and dignity of the individual members of the school community. In exercising justice there is a balance to be struck between what will be for the good of all and what is due to the individual. Neither the good of all nor the rights of the individual are absolute. Justice seeks for a proper proportionality.

Youngsters, particularly at the primary level, are less likely to talk about justice than fairness, for which children generally have a keen sense. 'That's not fair, miss' is a cry that has echoed through most classrooms. If there has been a serious act of misbehaviour warranting some form of sanction or punishment, children usually fully understand this. Getting away with it may bring momentary satisfaction but overall it is known that this is not fair. But neither is disproportionate punishment of the individual or punishment of the whole class when everyone knows there were only one or two culprits.

Behaviour policies, school rules and the way they are administered should reflect a basic fairness. How far are such policies based upon a Christian understanding of justice?

The coalition government that came to power in Britain in 2010 made fairness a keyword in its policies. It provoked considerable debate about just what fairness means and how it should be seen in practice at a time of radical cuts in public spending. Many feared it would prove to be a fine word with little content – especially for those at the bottom of the pile. A Twitter message sent in to the *Today* programme suggested the following as a definition of fairness: 'The opportunity to spend my money on my son's education so that he might have an unfair advantage over others!' Another contributor to the discussion made a distinction between fairness and justice, suggesting that in matters of justice all members have a greater say in what constitutes 'the just' and in the processes that ensure just outcomes. There is a deeper public involvement and a greater commitment.

The root idea of justice in the Scriptures centres on conforming to an agreed standard – initially a standard of measurement. Those who gave false measure or light weight were seen to be failing in justice. This was extended by implication to matters of behaviour; the just person was one who behaved according to expected codes of conduct. The expectation to 'do justly' derived from the belief that God was just in all his dealings, and therefore what God did and commanded was both just and right (righteous). His expectation of human beings was to act similarly; at one level, the just person was the one who kept all that God had commanded.

At a deeper level, justice is more a matter of art than science, the product of wisdom rather than the rule book. In some legal judgments we are reminded that while the law may have been upheld, justice suffered. There was no rule book that told Solomon what to do when two women, each claiming to be the mother of the same child, asked him to judge between them (1 Kings 3:16-28). 'All Israel heard of the judgement that the king had rendered; and they stood in awe of the king, because they perceived that the wisdom of God was in him, to execute justice' (v. 28). In the days of the monarchy in Judah and Israel, one of the major tasks of the king was to exercise justice, especially ensuring that the rights of the vulnerable – the widows, orphans and foreigners – were protected. The prophets often censured the rich and powerful for their lack of justice and Amos declared that God was more interested in justice than in religious ritual and sacrifice (Amos 5:21-24). 'Take away from me the noise of your songs; I will not listen to the melody of your harps. But let justice roll down like waters, and righteousness like an ever-flowing stream' (vv. 23, 24).

God was thus seen to be the source of justice, his rule being righteous and just. In judging moral and religious failure God was seen to be just – he acted with justice, punishing evil and rewarding goodness. But his justice went beyond a tally in a ledger book. At the heart of the Christian notion of justice is the conviction that it does not dismiss or even destroy evil but transforms it.

The cross is central to an understanding of a divine justice that goes beyond rights and deserts and includes mercy and compassion, sacrificial love enabling the reordering of a world broken by wrong. The prophet Isaiah saw God both as just (righteous) and as saviour (Isaiah 45:21). It is in his justice, not in spite of it, that he saves.

This was what the Christian Church came to see as expressed and made real in the life, death and resurrection of Jesus. Such an understanding of justice neither denies the reality of wrongdoing nor underplays the consequences of evil, but it believes that the vicious circle of wrongdoing, punishment, guilt and condemnation is broken. At the same time, justice is more than simply dealing with what goes wrong. It is the positive action that ensures that the dignity and worth of individuals is upheld, most especially when they have little power or voice by which to maintain it themselves.

The parable in Matthew's Gospel (20:1-16) of the landowner who hired workers in the marketplace, agreeing a fee for a day's work but later taking on more workers and ending up paying everyone equally, including those who had worked for only an hour, is really about God's generosity rather than fairness. It is more about salvation than terms and conditions. But the fairness of such payments has certainly been questioned – as indeed the workers who had toiled all day questioned it. What the parable does is place fairness in a larger context than simply a matter of mathematical equality or a ledger book calculation of what people deserve. Grace and generosity have their own effect upon what might normally be seen as fairness and justice.

In both small and bigger ways, justice is a constant issue in the classroom and the life of a school. It lies behind the right of each pupil to receive an educational experience related to their personal gifts and needs. Differentiation is not simply a question of raising standards; it is also a matter of justice. But all teachers know there is a balance that has to be kept between meeting the demands of a particular individual and ensuring the well-being of the whole class.

There is clearly a sharp issue of justice when it comes to the matter of exclusions. The exclusion of a particular individual may be strongly argued for on the basis of the advantages this will have for the rest of the class, not to mention a reduction in stress levels for the teacher. But the implications for the individual should also be considered and, as already indicated, there are a number of church schools where there is an explicit decision not to exclude any pupil. They adopt strategies that are believed to more fully reflect the Christian understanding of justice and transforming forgiveness.

Governors are sometimes required to take hard decisions on staffing matters that result in either capability procedures or redundancy. There are, of course, significant educational and financial aspects to such matters, but in the carrying out of the necessary procedures there are clear issues of justice that will exercise the wisdom and judgement of the governors. Some head teachers in church schools have gone out of their way to devise imaginative ways of prioritising their budgets so that they do not have to make teachers redundant. And they have done so because of their views on justice and fair dealing. Obviously that is not always possible. Dwindling numbers and restricted budgets can mean there is no alternative. But the manner in which the redundancy process is carried out should itself reflect the Christian values of the school.

In the discussion of such matters as redundancy and disciplinary actions, governors in a church school should give thought to how a distinctively Christian view of justice might impact upon their decisions.

In fact, governors and head teachers need to consider how questions of justice impact on every aspect of the school's corporate life, be it in the distribution of resources, charging and remission policies, the taking up of CPD opportunities, admission policies, behaviour protocols, or the inclusion of pupil voices through school councils and the like.

There are many elements of the curriculum that evoke justice questions. Their exploration provides opportunities for teachers to indicate how a Christian understanding can contribute to the discussion of what are often extremely complex issues – legal, educational, political, economic, ecological. There may be times when we conclude that it all comes down to a simple matter of justice. The problem is that justice itself is seldom simple.

Forgiveness

Peter asked Jesus about forgiveness and wanted to know if he could be expected to forgive someone who had wronged him as many as seven times. 'Not seven times, but, I tell you, seventy-seven times', Jesus replied (Matthew 18:22), or 'seventy times seven', indicating that there should no end to forgiveness. He then went on to tell a story about a king who wished to settle accounts with his slaves (Matthew 18:23-34). One of them had no way of repaying the debt and appealed to the king on bended knee. The king had pity on him and forgave the debt, whereupon the slave went out, grabbed a fellow slave who owed him a small amount, and had him thrown into prison. When this was reported to the king he became very angry that one whose large debt had been forgiven had failed to show pity on a fellow slave even though his debt was small.

Jesus was teaching his disciples about the great forgiveness of God and the way they, as forgiven people, should also forgive others. This has been a profound underlying truth in Christian spirituality – we are neither blameless people, nor written-off people; we are forgiven and, as such, have a moral and spiritual duty to forgive others. But there is a kind of virtuous circle in this: as a forgiven person I am called to forgive others, and as a person willing to forgive others I am more aware of my own need for forgiveness. Hence the petition in the Lord's Prayer: forgive us our trespasses as we forgive those who trespass against us.

A distinction is often made between forgiving someone their fault and forgetting it. People sometimes speak as though forgiving is easy but forgetting is impossible. Those who have had to forgive really deep and penetrating wrongs, wrongs that have killed and wounded, maimed and traumatised, know all too well that forgiveness is not easy. It is demanding and is itself a form of sacrifice: the sacrifice of resentment and desire for revenge, the overcoming of anger and bitterness made all the more difficult when the wrong is not to you directly but to someone close to you.

There have been some famous acts of forgiveness, made in the limelight where their reality can be tested. One thinks of Nelson Mandela, of a father whose son had been killed in a terrorist bombing in Northern Ireland, and of a young man who, as a child, had witnessed the brutal murder of his family by the Khmer Rouge, survived by crawling out from under their dead bodies and many years later sought out the killers to forgive them. He did so having first become a Christian. Foundational in the Christian story are the words of Jesus from the cross: 'Father, forgive them; for they do not know what they are doing' (Luke 23:34). It is not just a matter of how many times one has to forgive; there is also the depth of the hurt to be forgiven.

Forgiveness seeks to restore relationships, broken and soured in the cycle of wrong and revenge. The ability to forgive may partly depend on a person's character – some have, we say, a forgiving nature. But it is more to do with an attitude developed through a habit of will. Having ourselves experienced forgiveness, having had the guilt of a wrong committed eased and our sense of worth restored, we are ourselves in a better place to be able to offer forgiveness to others. The example and support of others in this demanding experience of dealing with hurt and offering forgiveness is very important in the development of a forgiving way of life. The experience young people have within the school community plays an important part in the way they will behave and respond when they are hurt.

Church schools above all should be places that understand and exemplify what it means to be a community of forgiveness. In what ways is your school a place of forgiveness?

To be forgiving is not, of course, the same as condoning. The Christian understanding of forgiveness is interwoven with the demands of holiness and judgement. God's forgiveness is not a condoning of wrongdoing or an ignoring of its consequences. The cross takes seriously both the reality of wrong and the cost of forgiveness. The language of sacrifice emphasises this and ensures that evil is never underestimated. But the distinctiveness of the Christian faith is that the basis of forgiveness is through self-sacrifice. In Christ the cost to God of forgiveness is demonstrated and made real. Discipleship seeks to draw upon the grace, the Spirit, of God to enable the believer to face that demand for sacrifice, the self-giving that forgiveness calls for.

Forgiveness does not mean there is no place for judgement or punishment, but these are seen within the fuller context of what it is that will help to restore relationships and enable the wrongdoer to see what they have done, make amends and grow in maturity and goodness (holiness). Punishment is not revenge and in itself is not incompatible with that forgiveness that produces restored relationships.

Forgiveness is normally associated with wrongdoing, which is a moral or legal failure. But many of life's experiences of failure are neither moral nor legal. They are failures of ability, of knowledge, of skill, of aptitude. A school that is seeking, among other things, to help young people to grow and develop in their knowledge, skills and aptitudes will often be faced with failure – pupil failure and failure on the part of staff. If there is no failure there will be no growing. Young people need to be challenged if they are to develop to their full potential, and along the way there will be failures. It does no one any good to pretend this does not happen. The notion that there is no such thing as failure, only deferred success, is a dangerous nonsense. In an era where success and achievement mean so much and appear at times to be a matter of how many boxes can be ticked, being realistic about failure and believing that it can be transformed is counter-cultural. Church schools should be glad to be distinctive in this way.

Failing to achieve something – a spelling, a high grade in an exam, success in a sports event, is not the same thing as being a failure. No one should ever be treated or written off as a failure. A school that has as one of its priorities the enhancing of a person's worth will never do that.

The church school should be particularly skilled in dealing with failure because of its distinctive understanding of forgiveness, of the significance of relationships and of the worth of each individual. How far does your school, in its desire for success, have a positive view of failure?

Gratitude and generosity

Norman Wisdom, the comic actor, singer, film star and musician, died in 2010 aged 95. A programme in tribute to him drew, among other things, on the many interviews he gave on television. They revealed his inexhaustible energy and love of acting the fool, his rather anarchic character and teasing sense of humour. But they showed him too as a man of an amazingly generous and grateful character – amazing because the early years of his childhood had been so horrendous. Abused by a bullying father, abandoned by his mother, living on the streets from the age of 12, he had every reason to grow up embittered and cynical. Yet he genuinely expressed his gratitude for virtually every one of his experiences, even that of being thrown across the room and hitting the ceiling. He was grateful that it taught him how to fall! He does not seem to have had a bad word to say about anyone. That is remarkable, and demonstrates a graciousness in the human spirit that is able to rise above even the worst of backgrounds.

In the Christian understanding such graciousness is a gift of God, the working of the Spirit of grace in a person's life. It is the way of life that can be found in a gracious, grateful and generous community. That is what a church school should be.

Under the rule of God, within God's kingdom, gratitude is not a duty hard wrung from an unwilling heart. It is a 'holy habit' borne of an awareness of all that we have to be grateful to God for and all for which we can give thanks to others. The voice of worship begins with thanks and praise, as seen in Psalm 107:1, which – like many of the Psalms – begins by calling worshippers to an expression of gratitude: 'O give thanks to the Lord, for he is good; for his steadfast love endures for ever.'

Gratitude is borne of an acknowledgement that we are not self-sufficient individuals – we are creatures of God. We are interdependent, with needs that only others can fulfil. We are receivers of so much, not necessarily or even usually through what we deserve, but because of the generosity and efforts of others.

St Paul was always giving thanks: thanks to God for all that he had received through Christ, and thanks to those whom he visited and wrote to – thanks for their faith, their kindness, their perseverance. He called upon the Christians at Thessalonica to give thanks, not just in good times or when everything was going well, but in all circumstances (1 Thessalonians 5:18a). That is not easy, but to find something to give thanks for even in difficult times is good for the soul. It makes gratitude more than just a matter of warm feelings when things are fine. Such gratitude regardless of circumstances is distinctive in its grounding in the love and gracious generosity of God.

In what ways does your school express its thanks? Are there people who never get thanked? Are there circumstances for which it is felt thanks would not be appropriate?

A church school should be a place of gratitude – a place where saying thanks is not just a matter of good manners but a way of life, an attitude that values the contribution and efforts of others, whether that be of other pupils, of staff, of parents or of the community at large. Gratitude is an expression of the value we place upon what is done – the effort put in, the willingness to give up time for the benefit of others.

It is often said that we should be good givers. Jesus said that it is more blessed to give than to receive. And of course there is truth in that. Selfishness and possessiveness, which seek to keep everything to ourselves – our possessions, our time, our ideas – are not traits to be encouraged. But it is also important that we are good receivers – grateful and gracious in accepting what others offer, even, and indeed especially, if it is not perfect. Rejecting the gift, the efforts, of others is immensely damaging to their sense of worth. When Jesus noticed a widow putting just a few coins into the Temple treasury, a mere nothing compared to the offerings of the Pharisees and the wealthy, he commended her for her sacrificial generosity (Luke 21:1-4). When a young lad had just his small lunch pack to offer to Jesus when the crowds were hungry, Jesus accepted what was given, gave thanks, and it became a meal for everyone (Luke 9:12-17).

Such a gracious gratitude is itself an act of generosity, an openness to others that should be a prominent mark of a church school. Being inclusive in our dealings with others, open to views, attitudes, lifestyles different to our own, is valuable in its own right. It is not part of a church school's ethos simply in order to counteract the accusations of secularists that church schools are divisive and lead to social fragmentation. It is part of that giving worth to others that is central to the Christian understanding of how God treats us and how we should treat one another in order to promote their well-being and their development into full human beings.

Such generous openness of mind and heart is not be confused with a lack of conviction or a failure to make up our minds. It is part of that humility which admits that none of us has the full picture or all the answers. Those who are different to us, who disagree with our opinions, may well have insights we have failed to see and which we need in order to get a fuller picture. It is bigoted faith and views that are dangerous, not firm convictions that remain open to other perceptions.

Church schools should be places of confident conviction but also of generous and gracious openness, for this is the way of life in the kingdom. Does your school share this balance?

God's generosity, even to the point of apparent profligacy, is the underlying lesson Jesus offered in the famous parable of the sower (Mark 4:3-8). The early church turned this into a detailed allegory about the gospel and people's reactions to it but that is unlikely to have been its original meaning. The sower spreads seed all over the place even though some of it will fall on unpromising soil and in places where it may get choked by weeds. God's love is scattered all over – not restricted to where it is guaranteed to produce a harvest. There is an extravagant generosity about God.

Jesus taught that those who follow his way, who are members of the kingdom, should have a similar generosity – giving where there is no thought of return, giving for its own sake to those who cannot repay

(Luke 14:12-14). This should be reflected in, among other things, a school's approach to charities and helping the underprivileged of other countries.

Even more radically, Jesus said that we should give of ourselves, our love, to those who hurt us, who are our enemies (Luke 6:32-36). In a church school this way of behaving should not just be an idea taught in collective worship or in the classroom; it should be part of the way the school community conducts itself, not least in the corridors and playgrounds.

I am not suggesting that gratitude and generosity are values exclusive to church schools. As throughout this book, what is being suggested is that such values are given their Christian distinctiveness by being grounded in the Christian story – in the life and teachings of Jesus.

Truth and integrity

When he faced Pilate, his life at stake, Jesus declared that he had come into the world to testify to the truth and that everyone who belongs to the truth listens to his voice. Pilate asked: 'What is truth?' (John 18:37b, 38). Was this said in a dismissive tone to end an interrogation that Pilate had little taste for? Or was it a genuine enquiry, Pilate hoping that Jesus would enlighten him on a philosophical question that the best of minds have long puzzled over? There is no way of knowing, for Jesus gave no reply. If we want to know what John in his Gospel understands by truth then we have to read the many passages in which Jesus is reported talking about the truth.

Key to the Christian understanding are the words of Jesus recorded in John 14:6a: 'I am the way, and the truth, and the life.' The basic and distinctive understanding of truth is that it is not a proposition or a series of concepts – it is a person. This can sometimes be lost sight of amidst all the volumes of theology and dogmatics that have been produced, which so often feel abstract and distant. But it is on the person of Jesus that the Christian search for truth should focus.

The significance of Christian truth is that it is a quality of a whole person, not just a matter of truthful words. It is more to do with what is in the 'inward being' (Psalm 51:6a) than with what is simply on the lips. It is the characteristic of a human life lived in relationship with the one who is the Truth; in relationship with the source and goal of reality at its deepest. It is life lived in God's truth.

In describing Jesus as 'without sin' Christians are not only stating something of the close, unbroken relationship between Jesus and God the Father, they are also making claims about the integrity of Jesus' human life. There is no flaw, no covering of the cracks in his person. He is whole, totally 'sincere' – a word that some people suggest comes from the idea of a piece of pottery that has no cracks, no flaws. A cracked pot needed wax (*cera*) to cover up the flaws and give the impression that it was perfect. A truly perfect pot was sincere – without wax. It was integrity that took Jesus to the cross – the determination to be true to himself and his mission rather than deny what he believed to be true, what he believed to be his calling, even if it cost him his life. Saints and martyrs, known and unknown, have followed that example. John the Baptist had the same integrity and it cost him his life too. He preached his message fearlessly, unswayed by the pressure that religious and political leaders put upon him. He was no reed blowing in the wind (Luke 7:24b).

This truth of person, integrity, is seen in the correlation between what Jesus said and what he did. By contrast, some of his sharpest words were addressed to the Pharisees and religious leaders, who said fine things but did not live up to their words. They were hypocrites.

Do the actions of your governors and school's leadership reflect the fine words of your school's mission statement? Is there integrity in the life of your school?

It might be claimed that education is itself a search for and growth in truth – truth about oneself, about the world, and beyond. On the basis that God is truth and all that is true is congruous with such a God, there can be no predetermined limits for the search for truth. The modern atheistic/secular attacks on religion focus on views that appear to be in radical conflict with the findings of science. While it is true that there are Christians who resist the findings of science on dogmatic grounds, this is not true of mainstream Christianity and certainly not of that form of Christian understanding that the majority of the Church of England represents. National statements relating to education in church schools, both from the bishops and from the National Society, make it clear that schools should not only be inclusive but should never seek to limit the search for truth on the basis of fundamentalist literalism.

As mentioned earlier, the Church does not always come out well on this matter historically, having opposed both Galileo and Darwin, among others. While recent years have seen a rise in conservative Christianity that is again widening the gulf between science and religion, more people these days do seem to accept that there does not have to be that kind of conflict between science and religion. This is partly because the distinctive contribution each makes in the search for truth is more readily recognised. Genesis and cosmology are not in conflict because they are concerned with different things. Science and religion have different starting points and explore different questions using different kinds of language.

Church schools should be confident in opening up the big questions that religion poses concerning what life is about, what death means, how we account for illness and disaster, and whether there is life beyond this one. The discussion of areas of scientific understanding and the way that knowledge has been put to technical application should not be off limits to students. These have implications for religion, and faith will take a stance on issues arising from both.

There should be every encouragement to discuss such moral issues as the point at which human life begins, whether euthanasia is ever justified, and life-and-death decisions made in the face of limited resources. A fuller understanding of truth draws upon the insights of both faith and science, and at times is willing to hold them in an unresolved tension.

What implications in terms of the curriculum are there for a church school seeking to encourage an exploration of truth that includes both a religious and a scientific viewpoint?

Truthfulness is, of course, very important and it is to be hoped that all schools seek to encourage it in their pupils and students. It is just as important that there is truthfulness among staff and governors. Obviously there are times when confidentiality means there cannot be total openness. Individuals have the right to expect protection in matters of personal information. Similarly, governors cannot always keep parents informed of developments until their outcome is clear. This is often the case, for example, in relation to staffing issues. Data protection requirements and human resources protocols have to be observed.

But these are the exceptions. In other circumstances it is important that there should be honest communication and integrity about such things as assessment and statistics of achievement. In a culture of league tables, where a school's future, let alone its reputation, can depend on the public perception of its performance, there are certainly temptations for teachers, heads and governors to be economical with the truth. A church school's integrity, however, should be beyond question, its communication open and truthful. That is not always easy. For example, when a school goes into special measures and the inspection report indicates criticism of the leadership and governance of the school, the temptation is to become defensive and elusive. But how can young people learn honesty and integrity if the adults in the community do not act with truthfulness.

Hope

Dipping pens were still being used when I was at primary school. A friend of mine unfailingly managed to get great blots of ink all over his exercise book. Giving him a new book, our teacher once said to him: 'I hope you'll be able to keep the blots out of this book, Kevin.' He looked at her with amused resignation: 'Some hopes, miss,' he said.

Schools should be outstanding places of hope. And church schools should be supremely hopeful communities. Is that how you see your school?

Hope isn't wishful thinking – something Kevin clearly thought his teacher was indulging in. It is the expectant looking for a good outcome that still lies in the future, as yet unrealised, as yet unseen. In his letter to the Romans St Paul states that 'hope that is seen is not hope. For who hopes for what is seen?' (Romans 8:24b). In the Christian faith the great hope is salvation, both for individuals and for the whole of creation, transforming the brokenness of the present situation into a harmony and wholeness that is the kingdom of God. It is a hope grounded in the promise of God and in his action through and in Jesus Christ. In the words of Julian of Norwich, it is the belief that 'all will be well, all will be well and all manner of things will be well' – not just because that is what we would like to be the case but because there is good reason to believe that God intends it to be so.

Hope does not have a guaranteed outcome and in some circumstances it can appear to be very foolish. The families of the 33 miners trapped underground in a mine in Chile in the summer of 2010 spent 18 days praying and hoping that all would be well. As time went by, that faith and hope must have been sorely tested. Common sense gave little prospect of finding the men safe and well after so long underground. Once it was discovered they had survived, their families set up camp on the mountain beside the pit and waited, trusting that the huge technical problems of bringing the men out safely would be resolved. A hope founded on faith was interwoven with a hope grounded in the possibilities of human ingenuity, tenacity and courage. It was hope in God, in the rescuers, and in the resilience of the human spirit of the miners themselves. Not until all the men had emerged safely was that hope realised. Hope gave way to celebration, for the families, for the nation, for the watching world. Sadly there have been other disasters in which families and miners have also hoped but had their hopes dashed. Such was the case just a few weeks after the Chilean rescue when 29 miners in New Zealand perished.

The Christian hope for salvation in the future is matched with a hope in the power of God's Spirit at work in and with the human spirit now, to enable the transformation of lives from failure to success, from wrongdoing to goodness, from desperation to aspiration. It is hope in the processes of development and growth, nurtured, guided and challenged through the provision of inspiring (inspiriting) education. At its heart this is a spiritual matter but it is worked out in the everyday decisions and practices that make up the life of a school community. Hope as a kingdom value is not only what happens in a moment of crisis but what informs the whole of life.

A church school should be a place that lives and breathes hope – hope in God's transforming power, hope in the gifts and abilities of all who play their part in the life of the school, hope in the power of the school to develop the potential of all its members.

Hope is not a whistling in the wind, it is a habit of positive expectation and action that is excited by and celebrates the possibilities of young lives.

In this chapter I have tried to give an indication of some of the Christian/kingdom values that should permeate a church school's Christian ethos and of how they gain their distinctive character through the basis they have in beliefs about God and in the story of Jesus. It is not an exhaustive list.

Governors may like to suggest and explore what other values they would include in a list of the core values that build up the ethos of their school, relating them to the Christian story.

More than
Caring and
Sharing

SEVEN

The whole child matters

The 2004 Children Act was a direct response to the tragic events surrounding the death of Victoria Climbié. The Green Paper leading to the legislation was entitled *Every Child Matters* (ECM) and the ECM agenda has shaped much of the provision for children and young people in the years that followed.

The aims of the programme were set out under five headlines:

- be healthy
- stay safe
- enjoy and achieve
- make a positive contribution
- achieve economic well-being.

Underpinning this vision for improvement in the outcomes for children and young people lay a radical change in the way the whole system of children's services worked. Because the focus was on children, young people and their families rather than on organisations, it was decided that there needed to be integration of the relevant statutory agencies and much closer partnership with voluntary and faith groups. The concept of the Extended School was introduced, defined as 'one that provides a range of activities and services, often beyond the school day, to help meet the needs of children and young people, their families and the wider community'. Although this was sometimes misunderstood and teachers feared that it meant that schools should themselves provide all the services desired, such as childcare before and after the school day (it didn't mean this), the programme did give an added impetus to schools to be more fully involved in their local communities. More will be said of that later.

In a liberal free society you would be hard pressed to find someone who believes that every child does NOT matter. No one is likely seriously to advocate that children should not be healthy and safe, should not experience enjoyment and be able to achieve, should not make a positive contribution or achieve economic well-being. But general acceptance is not the same as total agreement and in this chapter I wish to offer a critique of the ECM agenda and aims, not because they are wrong but because they don't say enough. I do this from a Christian perspective in the hope that it might stimulate discussion among governors, staff and parents in our church schools as they seek to articulate what is distinctive about a church school. I am writing in the early months of the coalition government, and how ECM will fare is not entirely clear. There may be changes of emphasis and, in times of radical cost cutting, the way services are provided will certainly change. However, the points that the ECM agenda raise about what we seek to provide for young people in their development continue to be pertinent.

Every child matters

Yes, of course. Much of what has been written here already emphasises the significance of every child as an individual, made in the image of God. The fact that Christians believe every child matters to God places a duty of care upon everyone towards every child. But we need to go further. For what child is it that matters to God and therefore to those who have care of them in the education system? Is it the child seen as a potential adult whose worth is not in what they are now but in what they will be in the future? This is equivalent to the attitude sometimes found in church congregations where children are spoken of as 'the church of tomorrow', the implication being that they can reasonably be ignored today. Is the child that matters a statistic in assessment tables reflecting the teacher's achievement, a potential economic unit, a future producer of services or goods? Taken as a whole it looks as if ECM has at least half an eye on the child as a future employee and economic factor.

It is the whole child that matters

It does matter that every child matters – the able and the strong, the disadvantaged and the disabled, the gifted and the talented, those with special needs. There should be no discrimination by race, gender, orientation, faith, ability, age, language. Differentiation, yes, but not discrimination. But, in addition, it matters that the *whole* child matters.

Church schools should have a special concern for the whole child – physically, emotionally, socially, morally, intellectually and spiritually.

Different pedagogies place different emphasis upon the significance of individual differentiation with personalised programmes of learning, and the place of learning together in groups. In most schools there is no doubt a healthy balance of the two. If the individuality of a child or young person is not recognised, fostered, supported and challenged then they are not being treated as though they matter. But individuality is not the same as isolation, and the social, cultural and relational context that helps to shape an individual also needs to be taken into account. At one level this impacts upon how a school involves parents and carers in the total life of its community. Few schools these days keep parents at a distance – literally beyond the school gate and without appropriate communication. But it is not always recognised just how daunting school can still be to some parents – especially if their own school experience was less than positive. Caring for the whole child means taking into account the familial and social networks that impinge upon each pupil or student. Some schools emphasise this by creating formal partnerships with parents together with contracts on specific issues such as homework. Parents' associations can also help to create this sense of working together.

Spirituality

Although the language of spirituality is widely used these days it can be so vague and generalised that it is not easy to determine exactly what is meant by it. Because it has long been associated with religious faith it is assumed that church schools will automatically be places where what is spiritual is understood and promoted. My own experience leads me to believe that governors and staff sometimes find it difficult to articulate what they mean by spirituality, although they consider it important.

Foundation governors might initiate a discussion in the governing body and among staff on the meaning of spirituality and how it is or could be encouraged and explored in their school.

If human beings are spiritual as well as physical, emotional, moral, social and intellectual then it is part of what makes up a 'whole' person and should be included in their education. At its simplest the spiritual includes a sense of otherness beyond the immediate and physical; an other that not only exists but can in some way be related to. It includes the sense of wonder and creativity, of awe and excitement, working more often through the imagination and intuition than through the rational. It enhances experience through what is perceived as the transcendent. Spirituality is an appreciation and cherishing of what is good, joyful, truthful and beautiful, and, in relationship with others, of what is generous, creative, loving. The spirit of a person is seen in acts of courage and perseverance, in dealing with both setbacks and praise, in endeavour and enquiry.

The human spirit, no less than the physical body, has needs that have to be met if it is to be healthy and develop. At root there is the need to be loved and to love, to feel worth and appreciation, to have opportunities for giving as well as receiving, to have a sense of belonging. The spirit will not flourish if it does not have the opportunity to be stimulated and express itself – be it through art, through writing, through music, through dance, or through physical activity. Religious faith believes that the spirit also needs to be supported through opportunities for what has been described as 'devotional spirituality' – individual and corporate prayer, worship, reflection and contemplation.

What opportunities can you provide to help children flourish spiritually? What evidence have you seen of such flourishing in individual children?

All matter

It is both inevitable and right that the emphasis has been upon the child. If a school loses that as its primary focus things are going badly wrong. But when we consider the responsibilities governors and others have for a school it is important that attention is also given to the whole school community. So, as far as a school is concerned, it is not only that the whole and every child matters but that the whole and every person of the school matters.

Teaching staff, TAs, admin staff, caretaking, cleaning and catering staff – all matter. So do parents and carers and those who volunteer from the community to assist with learning and activities, accompany trips, help raise funds, form work parties. There is a responsibility, in some instances enshrined in law, for their safety, their well-being, their sense of achievement, an acknowledgement that they make a difference. Proper care goes beyond what the law demands.

The provision of and encouragement to undertake professional development is both a way of caring for the individual staff member and necessary for the school as an effective institution. This is readily understood by most governing bodies though they are sometimes less aware of their own needs for training and updating. What can be underestimated is the need for succession planning and the way in which staff development enables this. No governing body is keen to lose an excellent senior teacher or deputy. At worst there can be a kind of possessiveness which, in seeking to hang on to a staff member, discourages appropriate development; e.g. NPQH, the qualification for headship. This is a form of selfishness and in the long run is very short-sighted. A church school whose ethos includes values of service and sacrifice should always be willing to look beyond its own immediate needs to those of the wider education world. At a time when small rural schools are often struggling through declining numbers and tight budgets, partnerships and federations may be a necessary way forward if they are to survive.

When 'stronger' schools are asked to consider partnering a more vulnerable school, the church school can reflect its distinctive ethos by asking not 'What are we going to get out of it?' but 'What can we offer to the partnership?'

Healthy

Although the most famous, Jamie Oliver – whose comments about the quality of school meals were not always popular – has certainly not been the only person to campaign for healthy food for schoolchildren. Catering services have responded, although, sadly, children and parents haven't always followed suit. In too many schools the number of school dinners purchased has declined following the introduction of more nutritious meals. Fruit has also been made available for children during the day. Various initiatives have encouraged children to grow vegetables that are then made part of their meals. There has been renewed interest in cooking for healthy diets.

Activity and fresh air have also been made part of the curriculum, not least for Early Years. The ancient dictum that healthy bodies make for healthy minds (*mens sana in corpore sano*) clearly has its modern proponents.

In the Christian tradition there is a linguistic relation between health and wholeness, and this reinforces what has already been said about concern for the whole person. St Paul writes of the body being a temple, something to be respected and not dishonoured. His primary concern was sexual purity but the teaching has wider implications and highlights a positive approach to physical well-being, not least in relation to spiritual health.

In a world that is increasingly 'noisy', not only with sound but also with data and information, where job requirements and consumer expectations set up ever greater demands, where poverty creates increasing vulnerability, the 'stresses' of everyday life can be a burden. Children and students also speak of stress in the face of SATs and GCSEs. The resilience to face this is in part a spiritual gift – developed through the ability to make use of quietness, reflection and meditation. Opportunities for reflection and quiet should be part of the everyday experience of pupils and students, available most obviously, but not only, in the context of collective worship.

The promotion of physical health is a proper concern in a church school, understood in terms of the healthiness (the wholeness) of the whole person in the context of a 'healthy', cared-for environment.

Safety and security

Given the background to the Every Child Matters programme in the Victoria Climbié case it is not surprising that safety was the first aim. Schools have a proper responsibility to ensure that the children and young people in their care are safe. It is a priority for Ofsted inspectors, and inspections have been stopped as soon as it became apparent that a school had shortcomings in its safeguarding and safety policies and procedures. Children must be kept safe from interference and unnecessary harm. Proper assessments have to be made of risks – from people, from the school environment itself, from activities that take place beyond the school during the school day. Although some people still complain if asked to undertake a safeguarding (CRB) disclosure, the requirement is both legally binding and best practice.

Governors have a responsibility to ensure that their school provides appropriate sex and drugs education and that it knows how to access the relevant support and counselling agencies as required. Recent reports on drunkenness among teenagers and even the very young indicate that there is also the need for education concerning the effects of alcohol. Such education is more than a knowledge of facts; it involves a consideration of the nature of relationships and personal responsibility that each of these topics involves.

There is a proper discussion to be had when it comes to the assessment of what is considered to be reasonable risk. Much fun is made of the alleged requirements of Health and Safety that go beyond common sense and into the realms of the ridiculous. Many supposed regulations were, in fact, myths. But not all. To an older generation that enjoyed the thrill of sliding across playgrounds on icy mornings, the caution of schools that close after half an inch of snow can appear excessive. But to the parent whose child broke a leg because no salt was put down, the matter looks different. Wearing goggles and a hard hat can seem to take away the whole enjoyment of a game of conkers – unless your daughter had lost an eye in such a game. It is inevitable, not least in an age of increasing litigation, that those who bear responsibility err on the side of caution while others complain that we are increasingly becoming a nanny state.

School leaders and governors often have to weigh up conflicting issues. On the one hand, they have a responsibility towards the children and young people in their care, while, on the other, a school should be a place where children and young people grow in the sense of their own responsibility and decision making.

From a Christian viewpoint the emphasis might be better focused on security than on safety. At a basic level, children should be secure in the environment of the school. In one school, for example, a low fence around the Early Years' outside learning area next to a public roadway presented a security risk. A child could be easily lifted over the fence, so the governors decided that a higher wall should be built. It is normal practice in most schools for either the outside main door or an inner door to be secured by a code lock. All visitors have to sign in and wear a badge. Personal data and records are also properly required to be kept secure, both physically and in confidence.

But of deeper significance is the inner security that should be developed as part of a child's right. Such a security relates to what has been mentioned many times already, namely, a sense of worth grounded in the experience of being loved and giving love. This security embraces the whole person – physical, emotional, socially, morally, intellectually and spiritually. Such security makes the taking of risk both appropriate and possible.

There is **physical risk**, which is basic to undertaking challenging activity. In infancy, learning to walk is itself a risky business – there are sure to be falls. Without risking that, no child would ever learn to stand on its own two feet and walk. This is clearly a challenge and it can produce anxiety. But with appropriate support and encouragement the challenge is met and the delight on the face of an infant who has managed a few steps is evidence of the sense of achievement, in spite of the bumped knees. At every stage of development there are similar physical challenges, and without taking a well-managed risk the desired progress would not take place.

There is **emotional risk**, required of those who love and are loved, who offer service without counting personal cost, who have the courage to search their own hearts and character. The heartaches of young love are a common and necessary part of growing up, and few avoid them in their teenage years. But it is not only in romantic attachments that there is risk. Friendship offered and scorned or betrayed is equally painful – for young children as for adults. Judas' betrayal must have been devastating to Jesus but so too was the fact that all the disciples left him when he was arrested and the boastful Peter denied having ever known him. The simple act of offering a gift is itself a risk: the risk of it being rejected, the risk of it being something the other person does not like. There is also risk involved in being willing to search one's own heart, being honest about oneself – risk that in a religious setting calls for an honest act of confession.

Social risk is demanded of those who move out from their familiar circle of friends and context to engage with people of other cultures, lifestyles and background. There is not only the risk of feeling uncomfortable or embarrassed but the risk of actually hurting others

simply by not knowing the norms of their way of life, their beliefs, their culture. The diplomatic service puts diplomats newly arrived in foreign countries through a series of role-plays to help them learn and avoid cultural *faux pas*, but the first embassy social event is still a risk. Changing school may itself feel like a considerable risk, with new norms to learn, relationships to make. Inter-school visits at points of transition can help alleviate the worst of the anxieties but not eliminate the risk.

There is **intellectual risk** involved in questioning accepted ways of understanding and exploring insights that move a person out of their comfort zone. All new learning involves this to a lesser or greater extent. It entails the risk of not being able to understand or cope with new work, and the fear that it may disturb previously held viewpoints. Ordinands at theological college sometimes find studies in biblical criticism threatening to their beliefs about the nature and authority of Scripture. The requirements of the school RE syllabus, which insist on the study of religions other than Christianity, can sometimes present difficulties for those who do not wish to question their own faith position. But such risk is required of those who are willing to open their minds to wider knowledge and wisdom. Advances in scientific knowledge would not have been achieved if the current orthodoxy had not been questioned. One has only to look at the story of Galileo to realise that the risks, as well as the rewards in terms of new knowledge, can be considerable.

Spiritual risk is experienced in the search for an inner truth beyond accepted beliefs and dogmas, worship and religious practices. This will often involve the uncomfortable challenge of facing doubt when what we want is certainty. For those who have never allowed themselves to spend time reflecting in quietness, allowing the power of silence to surround them, such stillness can feel like a risk. TV programmes, such as *Silence*, on the experience of visitors to monasteries or those who undertake a Trappist discipline, bear witness to the anxieties

experienced. Those involved felt that in opening up to such silence they were risking something of themselves at quite a deep level – a risk they found worth taking.

In a world where young people seem to be wedded to their ear plugs, constantly listening to chat or music, silence can feel a risk or a nonsense. To experience what it might offer, they will need to be given the opportunity to take the risk. There should be provision of quiet spaces, both within the school and in the grounds. Prayer is a vital aspect in the development of personal spirituality, and while there is need for sensitivity when inviting children to pray, a church school should feel confident in providing opportunities for prayer both corporately and individually. Such opportunities should extend beyond the sharing of prayer within an act of collective worship.

The Christian individual and community believe that a strong sense of inner security that allows for risk is a gift of God, made available through the loving acceptance of those with whom we have contact.

Church schools will seek to be communities of an accepting love that encourages and supports individuals through the taking of such risks, knowing that, as with all risk taking, the outcome will sometimes be painful as well as exciting.

Jesus did not simply risk questioning the religious orthodoxy of his day and the authorities who supported the status quo, but risked his trust in God to the point where it felt that the Father had deserted him. There is no more haunting cry than that of the man on the cross: 'My God, my God, why have you abandoned me?' And there is no deeper example of the trust that arises from a profound security than the final words: 'Into your hands I commit my spirit.'

Achieve and enjoy

Achievement is not simply a matter of abilities. It requires the opportunity for those abilities to find expression in circumstances that may be challenging but not overwhelming. Nor is enjoyment of achievement simply a matter of being able to do something. The repeated achievement of a task that is too simple creates boredom and frustration, which is counterproductive to learning. Teachers are increasingly being required to demonstrate the professional skill of being able to differentiate the learning experience offered according to individual and group needs. This skill of accurate assessment is required not simply to satisfy data tables and statistical targets but to ensure that pupils and students neither have their confidence undermined by tasks far beyond their knowledge and ability nor are left unchallenged by tasks that underestimate what they can do. For young people to have their aspirations raised there is a need to present them with both challenge and opportunities for achievement. And the same is true of teachers.

St Paul knew that, in his terms, it was unwise to give the very young in faith the strong meat of demanding teaching but he was disappointed in those of his congregations who remained satisfied with spiritual 'milk'.

Governors have responsibility, together with the school leadership team, for target setting and monitoring pupils' achievement at each Key Stage and at in-between points, to ensure that each pupil and student is reaching appropriate levels of achievement and that the teaching is supporting progress. Where that is not so, additional support and intervention will be necessary. Some governors may feel that this is all a modern 'fad' involving unnecessary bureaucracy, but in reality such procedures are necessary tools to help ensure that every child receives the educational provision to which they are entitled. Used properly, such data lead not to a reduction of each child to a statistic but

to a way of ensuring that each one is viewed individually and that none gets lost.

A teacher friend of mine used to complain bitterly whenever the cry went up among youngsters that they were bored. What he was complaining about was their lack of imagination and creativity, their unwillingness to take upon themselves responsibility for their learning and for developing activities they would enjoy. He was a good teacher and no doubt spent a great deal of his time ensuring that the learning experience was meaningful, related to young people's interests and ways of learning, and affording the opportunity to set their own targets. We may empathise with the frustration in his complaint, but the reality is that young people can feel bored, and there will be times when what has to be learnt will not immediately appear to be relevant, exciting or even particularly interesting.

The world for which young people are being prepared will not always prove enjoyable or best use an individual's abilities. Certain qualities are needed to cope with what is not enjoyable, or with frustrated achievement, if the child is not to become cynical, disillusioned or despairing. A church school – coming from a position of faith in which endurance and hope are significant values – may well feel it has something particular to offer in tackling how this might be achieved.

One of the problems is that learning requires a degree of patience – on the part not just of teachers but of learners too. A youngster longing to be able to play complicated tunes on the piano will seldom enjoy the sessions practising scales and only after some time find that the dexterity and disciplined finger movement this has provided pays off, making the ability to play the tunes the more enjoyable. Students have to show a degree of trust in their teachers that the

learning journey they are on has a worthwhile destination, even if some of that journey passes through a landscape that is demanding and not immediately rewarding. Skills and knowledge take time to build up, but while it is unhelpful to try to run before we can walk, it is equally inappropriate to force a person only to walk when they have reached the point where they need the challenge of running.

Schools can develop a culture of achievement that supports those with ability but leaves others behind. Some schools have achieved specialist status in certain subjects, with government encouragement to do so. This has no doubt had some good effects on student achievement and a school's own sense of success. But there clearly are cases where an emphasis upon, for example, sport or academic achievement has left behind those who are not 'sporty' or academically gifted. The notion that in such cases there should be differentiation (selection) at admission remains controversial.

Those who achieve well, in whatever area of learning, should not be blind to the abilities of others. A proper sense of one's own worth includes an appreciation of the gifts of others and of the efforts of those with less ability. That may be a hard and sophisticated lesson for young people to learn, not least because there are plenty of adults who have not learnt it. But in a society that truly seeks to care for all its members, such lessons are important. Governors should review their SEN policy and monitor the effectiveness of the school's integration of SEN pupils.

Schools have always found ways of acknowledging in public the success of their pupils. What they choose to celebrate and the way they do this gives out significant messages about the culture and ethos of a school. In one school, only the names of those students who have gone to university get displayed while in another the only photos of former students on display are of those who achieved county level or higher at a sport. This is no more desirable than it would be in a church school for only those who achieve well in RE to be celebrated. Part of the enjoyment of the achievement of learning is its celebration by others – whatever the achievement, whatever the learning. The Pauline picture of the body with its many members, all interdependent and contributing to the whole, is important here.

Church school governors should consider the school's policy for celebration, ensuring that the achievements of all are recognised.

A school's responsibility goes beyond the current learning experience of its pupils and students. Learning, and the habit of learning, is not confined to school years. Part of what schools seek to do is to encourage an awareness that learning is a lifetime matter – not least in an employment market where it is likely that employees will change jobs a number of times in their career, requiring the learning of different skills and knowledge bases. This places upon the school and the advisory services a considerable responsibility when children consider the choices they can make about future subjects to study or what further learning experience they will undertake beyond school, be it sixth-form college, learning at work, FE college, university or apprenticeship.

As important as achievement is, along with how to enable it and how to celebrate it, there is always the issue of what to do about failure to achieve, both wilful and unintentional. I am convinced that, in handling failure, the church school has resources within the Christian story for a distinctive approach, as already indicated in the section on 'Success and failure' in chapter 3.

Positive contribution

A once very active woman I knew had become increasingly disabled as she grew older, and whereas she had formerly been always on the go she was now confined to a wheelchair in an eighth-floor flat. She feared she was useless. 'All I ever do,' she said, 'is sit here and people pop in and we have a chat.' She wasn't aware of just what those 'chats' meant to the people who visited her. Her ability to listen and offer the occasional wise word had eased burdens, quietened anxieties, brought hope to a whole range of people. The local church also appreciated her daily prayers. Yet, compared to all that she had done in the past, she felt she had nothing to offer, was making no contribution to the community of which she was so much a part.

Making a positive contribution depends, in part, on abilities, but it is much more to do with an inner self-knowledge and self-confidence supported by those good relations that encourage a sense of self-worth. To be able to offer a viewpoint, an action, a service, a skill which will benefit others is part of what it means to 'love one's neighbour'. But if there is not a proper sense of love of oneself coming from a degree of self-knowledge and acceptance of who and what one is, then making a contribution that is felt to be positive will be hard. It is important, therefore, that schools assist their young people to reflect on who they are, how they differ from others, what it means to be significant as an individual, without them becoming unbearably self-absorbed. It is not only teenagers who face identity angst, through which they need to be supported, although the added hormone activity of teenage years certainly heightens that experience.

A church school should be particularly well placed to encourage not only a love of God and neighbour, but also a proper love of self, which is the basis for an appropriate self-confidence and without which making a positive contribution is difficult.

It is to be hoped that children and young people not only know they are making a contribution but are aware that it is appreciated. For this to happen the youngsters certainly need a degree of self-confidence and a sense of their own worth but they also need to be part of a community that opens up opportunities for them to make a contribution and then shows its appreciation. If this is to be the experience of every child, including the shy and the SEN, the gifted and talented and those lacking in confidence and with a poor sense of their own worth, then the community members, fellow pupils and students, as well as adults, will need to be very open, accepting and generous. Young people are well aware if praise is inappropriate or inflated. Both the achievement and the praise need to be authentic. Appropriate appreciation and celebration should be the character, the ethos, of the school, the way it is all the time, not just on odd occasions. So it means that being open to the contribution of every child will be evident in the classroom, on the sports field, in drama and in the school's work for the wider community, locally and beyond. It will be the attitude of staff towards each other and of governors towards staff. It will be a necessary part of listening to the pupil voice – in the classroom and at school council.

As a school helps students to look to their future it will be important that they have the opportunity to consider what it is that makes for responsible citizenship, how the individual has a part to play within society, and the attitude they will take towards the rules and disciplines society imposes.

In a church school it will be particularly important that the voice of the 'dissenter', those who do not believe or who hold a faith position that is not Christian, is both heard and appreciated, not least in RE lessons.

Achieving economic well-being

Setting the achievement of economic well-being as a specific target within the Every Child Matters programme must reflect a certain viewpoint about what it is to be human, or at least what matters most about being an adult human being. It arises from a capitalist, consumer society. Since that is the society we live in, the benefits from which we are, for the most part, content to enjoy, this is hardly surprising. It is not necessarily cynicism to suggest that a government struggling to meet a large welfare benefit bill seems keen to promote an education programme aimed at equipping young people for employment and keeping them off state welfare. The vast majority of people want to work, want to earn enough to feel reasonably comfortable. Achieving economic well-being is not just a matter of having the skills and knowledge through which to get a job, but also of having the ability to manage one's money and an awareness of the responsibilities having money places upon a person. The education system should at least make this a possibility for as wide a range of people as possible.

Governors have a responsibility to provide a curriculum, especially for 14- to 19–year-olds, that is sufficiently broad based and in which provision is made for vocational training. All students should have access to good career advice and the needs of the vulnerable should be met.

The Christian tradition has had a positive view of work, even if the Genesis myth suggests that it was disobedience to the divine will that made work difficult. The Puritan work ethic, with its attendant dangers of overwork and a failure to appreciate the benefits for human well-being of recreation and enjoyment, is well documented. The labourer, we are told, is worthy of his hire (Luke 10:7). And the wilful avoidance of work is criticised in the writings of St Paul (2 Thessalonians 3:10-13). But what does a policy of enabling economic well-being make of a Jesus whose major contribution was to be found not in his years working as a carpenter but in the three years of wandering around the country teaching, preaching and healing? As far as we know, he was dependent on the charity of others, not least that of wealthy women.

Jesus' example, along with that of many others, provides good reason to pause and consider whether 'economic man and woman' is all that needs to be said about what young people should be encouraged to achieve. From the perspective of faith, not only is there much to be discussed concerning attitudes towards wealth and poverty, money and possessions, but also opportunity should be given for a critique of materialism and the consumer society.

As well as seeking to ensure a proper distribution of work so that the apostles, for example, were not overburdened with everyday administrative matters, the early church expected its members to be supportive of one another, contributing to those in need and providing emergency funds in times of special hardship. Underpinning its teaching on the use of personal possessions lay the ancient tradition of tithing – of giving a tenth of one's income to God in recognition of the understanding that all things come from God and 'of thine own do we give thee'. The generosity of God evokes a response of gratitude in the believer expressed through generous giving. Other faiths, such as Islam, also have clear teachings about the use of money, on the duty of charity and such issues as exacting interest on a loan.

If it is the whole person as well as every child that matters then economic well-being will not be the only target that a school will seek to achieve for its young people. The human character and spirit include much more than that. What opportunities should be given for the human character to develop and spirit to flourish are matters that each school should properly give thought to and governors consider, while being aware of local circumstances and particular needs. In such discussion, the church school has the insights of the

Christian story and tradition to guide it and the experience of the community of faith to draw upon.

Christian answers will not be shared by all, but a church school should have the confidence to live by what it believes and be open to the insights others bring.

More than
Caring and
Sharing

EIGHT

RE and collective worship

In recent years, at a time when religious faith has increasingly been a subject of considerable public debate, successive governments have asserted that Religious Education in schools is important. The DSCF Guidelines published in 2009 begin with this statement: 'Religious Education (RE) is a very important subject in the school curriculum, and the Government is keen to ensure that it is of a high quality for all pupils.'

RE's changing position

Historically, the position of RE has been rather mixed. As we saw in chapter 2, it was the churches, and especially the Church of England, that initiated the provision of mass education at the beginning of the nineteenth century. One of the motives was without doubt the opportunity to teach the faith based upon the Bible and the Catechism. Pupils received education in the Church of England's understanding of the Christian faith and they were nurtured in the Church's rites, practices and doctrines. The state provision of education through Board schools from 1870 onwards encouraged instruction in the Christian faith, but secular voices joined with those of non-Anglican Christians to ensure that it should not be denominational, catechetical or indoctrinatory. Through the Education Act of 1944, Religious Instruction (RI) was not only legally required but was the only subject that had to be taught. And it was seen in terms of

Instruction rather than *Education*. The syllabus was agreed at local level through an Agreed Syllabus Conference where the Church of England, non-conformist churches and the local authority had equal votes, and unanimous decisions were required. This was to ensure that in all maintained schools, other than voluntary aided, there should be a non-denominational approach to RI. This included the voluntary controlled schools. The voluntary aided schools were able to teach in accordance with the rites, practices and doctrines of the school's foundation.

RI that followed the Agreed Syllabus was mainly biblical in character, and by the 1970s this had raised considerable debate about its suitability. The work of people such as Ronald Goldman in the 1960s and Ninian Smart in the 70s resulted in teaching that was both more thematic and more focused upon 'readiness for religion' and the phenomena of religion. The emphasis had changed from *instruction in religion* to the broader concept of *religious education*. But RE lost its way somewhat in both state and church schools and there was generally a lack of confidence about the value of RE. This trend changed for the better in 1992 with the introduction of Ofsted and denominational inspections, which set expectations concerning schools' compliance with the law in relation to RE and collective worship. Since that time, RE has become increasingly popular, as is shown by the number of pupils taking GCSE and A level in Religious Studies. No doubt this was also largely due to changes in the way the subject was tackled, making it more relevant to the interests and concerns of young people and so raising its image in students' perception.

The law

Although there have been frequent attempts to remove RE and collective worship from the legal requirements placed upon a school, successive governments have retained the statutory position. At one level this can, of course, be seen as an imposition, but at a time when human rights have played an important part in the wider context of education, it is also possible to see it as the protection of a child's or young person's entitlement to explore the meaning and implications of faith. This would be unacceptable were it not for the legal provision (School Standards and Framework Act 1998) whereby parents have the right to withdraw their children from RE and collective worship, although comparatively few ever exercise that right. The right of withdrawal is balanced by the right of parents whose children attend a community school or voluntary controlled school to request RE according to a particular faith tradition, and the school is required to make provision for this; for example, through arrangements such as changes to the timetable whereby a pupil can attend the desired RE in another school. If it fails to do so, the Local Authority has to make the provision. Neither the school nor the LA is required to pay for such teaching or for associated resources. Nor is the school required to teach the alternative RE.

The Agreed Syllabus and National Framework

While RE is not part of the national curriculum and therefore is not subject to national statutorily prescribed attainment targets, programmes of study or assessment arrangements, it remains part of the required basic curriculum and must be provided for every pupil registered in a maintained school (apart from those who have been withdrawn by their parents), including students in secondary sixth forms. Until 2004, however, there was no nationally accepted standard for RE. Pressure, not least from the Church of England, resulted in the publication that year of a non-statutory National Framework to guide both Local Authorities and faith communities in what pupils should study in religious education.

In response to the National Framework, the Church of England published *Excellence and Distinctiveness: Guidance on RE in Church of England Schools* (October 2005). Its first recommendation was that governors in voluntary aided schools should adopt their locally agreed RE syllabus, so long as it was based on the National Framework, together with *Excellence and Distinctiveness*. Previously, many dioceses had devised their own syllabus and recommended to governors of aided schools its use rather than the LA's Agreed Syllabus. Where a diocese covered a number of local authorities each producing their own Agreed Syllabus there was something to be said for a diocesan syllabus for use in the whole diocesan family of aided church schools. However, the National Framework offered an opportunity for a new way of working that provided continuity across the sectors and effective partnership between the dioceses and local authorities. It has meant, for example, that there has been a more effective use of shared resources. Roman Catholic education authorities have continued to produce their own RE syllabus for use in their schools.

Excellence

As far as I am aware, no one has ever advocated that RE should be badly taught. The 2009 DSCF Guidelines declared the government to be keen to ensure that RE was of a high quality for all pupils. The Church of England (2005) made 'Excellence' one of its two key principles in offering guidance to church schools on the teaching of RE.

Excellent teaching requires excellent teachers. As we shall see, it also requires other things, but this is where it must start. And there are any number of excellent RE teachers – but not everywhere, and not always in church schools. There is a shortage of those who have specialised training in RE and, too often, willing but non-specialist teachers not only teach the subject but are subject leaders. In some cases this has no detrimental effect but clearly it is not a healthy position for RE as a subject. Less acceptable in general and in church schools in particular is the relegation of RE to a cinderella subject foisted on to reluctant teachers or TAs simply to meet the demands of the law. The Dearing

Report urged the Church at various levels not only to encourage Christians to consider teaching as a vocation but also to 'work for the greater recognition and status of RE teachers in all schools by the provision of an appropriate career structure and corresponding salary scales and resources' (*The Way Ahead*, p. 81). Anglican Church colleges were expected to play their part in this through the development of Certificates in Church School Studies and Religious Studies. Concerns about the place of RE have risen sharply with the government's announcement of the review of the national curriculum and with the emphasis upon the English Baccalaureate.

Just as parents can withdraw their children from RE so students over the age of 18 who are in full-time education may also request in writing that they withdraw from the RE provided, although strictly they should seek RE in some form. Teachers also have the right not to teach RE. However, church schools, in appointing to RE teaching posts, can require that the appointed candidate is not only suitably qualified but also Christian. Apart from this instance, a teacher's religious belief and willingness or not to participate in RE provision cannot be the basis for disqualification from employment or discrimination in terms of pay or promotion.

It is sometimes claimed that the quality of RE as an educational experience is reduced by the possibility of it becoming an opportunity for indoctrination by teachers strongly committed to their faith. The danger is real and has to be watched out for. But experience seems to indicate that far from Christian teachers abusing their position, they lean over backwards to ensure that they do not indoctrinate and are usually very open and inclusive in what they teach and the way they teach it. The fear of indoctrinating actually appears to have the effect of reducing the confidence with which Christian teachers feel able to speak about their faith at all. Diocesan advisers visiting church schools, including voluntary aided schools, are sometimes saddened to discover that even generally excellent teachers, who are very good at teaching other faiths, are both less well informed and less confident in teaching Christianity. The reasons for this may well be complex but foundation governors in particular should be able to spot this and talk it through sensitively with the teachers involved. Research also indicates that Christian students feel it is inappropriate to share their faith in the classroom context, while atheist students felt it was vital that questions of faith, and non-faith, should be discussed.

In making appointments head teachers and governors should give special attention to the appointment of high-quality RE teachers able to teach the Christian faith with confidence as well as in an open and inclusive way.

Even the best teachers will be hampered in delivering excellent RE if other factors are not also taken into account. RE should be given sufficient time in the week; the Church's national guidelines suggest that this should be at least 5 per cent of curriculum time. No doubt this is more readily applicable in the secondary school setting, especially when RE is taught as an exam subject. But where in primary schools RE is more interwoven with other subjects in a creative curriculum there is an even greater need to monitor that it is in fact given appropriate attention. While other religions should be given their proper place as set out in the syllabus, a church school should allow for up to three-quarters of the time available to be spent on Christianity.

Appropriate professional development is not only a teacher's right but should be expected of teachers. In smaller schools, budgets may place restrictions upon the amount of time that teachers can be released for daytime courses, and when this is the case it is understandable that training related to core subjects is given priority. But if RE is to have a central place in a church school, as it should do, then the professional development of RE teachers should have a high place and not be neglected.

The same is true with regard to RE resources – including books, DVDs and artefacts. The opportunity for out-of-school experience is also very important. Learning about a church, synagogue, gurdwara or mosque is impoverished if pupils are not given the learning opportunities offered by a visit to places of worship and meeting with members of the faith community with whom major issues such as God, death and morality can be discussed. Such visits, where practicable, are in fact part of the statutory requirement under the National Framework.

Foundation governors should ensure that RE is afforded up to 5 per cent of curriculum time and that they manage the budget in such a way that allows for good resources, opportunities for professional development in RE, and time for school visits to places of worship.

Distinctive

As an area of learning, excellent RE will not look greatly different whether in a church school or in a community school. The difference is more likely to be found in the general school context and ethos within which RE exists as a subject on the timetable. In a church school it should relate to the living faith of the school community, both informing that faith and being informed by it. To this extent it is not simply another subject of study but offers insights and values that relate to every part of the curriculum. It should therefore reflect the Christian character of the church school. *Excellence and Distinctiveness* put it this way: 'In developing the distinctive approach to RE shaped by the National Framework, schools should consider what lies at the heart of the Christian faith.' This is reflected in the earlier chapters of this book in which the nature of the Christian faith has been explored. It also means that, without proselytising, the church school should provide, through RE and in other ways, opportunities for a personal response to that faith – to the God it worships and to the person of Jesus, as well as ensuring a critical engagement with faith. RE should help children and young people to develop an understanding of why religion is a serious matter that is worth taking seriously.

To quote *Excellence and Distinctiveness* again: 'RE is key to fulfilling the purpose of a church school as described by the late Lord Runcie when he was Archbishop of Canterbury:

- to nourish those of faith
- to encourage those of other faiths
- to challenge those who have no faith.'

The document recognised that it requires skill and sensitivity to maintain the balance between these intentions, and that local circumstances will affect the way in which that can be achieved.

The church school, far from being a ghetto of Christian faith resistant to the exploration of other faiths and worldviews, should be sufficiently confident in its own faith position that it encourages exploration and open dialogue with other faiths, welcoming areas of common concern, and being realistic and sensitive about differences. It thereby contributes to inclusiveness and social cohesion.

The church voluntary aided school has a specifically distinctive aspect to its RE provision. It is required, through its foundation, to teach RE in a way that is in keeping with the distinctively Anglican character of the school, its beliefs and practices. This will reflect points made in earlier chapters concerning belief, not least in chapter 4, on the Church. Together with collective worship, RE should provide opportunities for exploration of the Church's year, and this should be evident in displays both in the classroom and around the school. RE should also offer insight into the structures and worship of the Church, and of the wider Anglican Communion, extending pupils' and students' understanding of the global nature of the Christian faith and the richness of tradition that this has evoked.

Excellence and Distinctiveness recommended that up to three-quarters of RE curriculum time should be given to Christianity. This presents a difficulty for some Agreed Syllabuses and at different Key Stages. Aided schools can, of course, adapt the syllabus to meet this recommendation but controlled schools do not have this option. There would have to be curriculum enrichment to ensure that the Christian content reached this level.

RE should provide not only learning *about* and *from* faith (the two key concepts in the National Framework) in ways that inform the mind but also opportunities that promote spiritual, cultural and moral development grounded within the Christian traditions while drawing upon the insights and creativeness of other faiths. In learning *from* religion pupils are encouraged and challenged to reflect on what they have learnt *about* a religion, relating it to their own views and faith position.

RE, like faith, should include the exploration of 'big questions'. This can be both challenging and sensitive, and a church school ought to be in a particularly good position to enable it to take place. The nature of faith is itself one such 'big question', and while the possibility of developing a confident faith should always be available, a church school should also be especially sensitive to questions of doubt. Pupils should have opportunities for reflection, quietness and prayer as part of their religious education in its broadest sense and in addition to the corporate experience of collective worship.

Well-taught RE has a considerable contribution to make to the personal development of students, and a church school's distinctive understanding of what it is to be fully human will be reflected in this (see chapter 4). It is important in church schools that special care is taken to ensure that RE is taught in such a way as to be inclusive of all, since this reflects the Christian understanding of the importance of all. Considerable work has been done on the spirituality of children with special needs, and teachers in church schools should draw upon this and the relevant resources.

None of this will be achieved if the leadership and management of the school is not itself clear about the way it views RE, the place it is given within the life of the school, and the way in which it reflects and relates to the school's vision statement. RE should be part of the school's regularly reviewed improvement plan and self-evaluation. The significance of this is explored further in the book's final chapter.

Collective worship

I once asked a group of sixth-formers in a church secondary school what they thought about school assembly (as they called it). 'Well,' one of them said, 'it's like this. We all troop into the school hall and have to keep quiet until all the teachers have arrived and then we worship the head master.' Knowing the school well I had some appreciation of what he meant. But clearly this is not what is meant by the legal requirement for all registered pupils to attend a daily act of worship that is wholly or mainly Christian in character.

The statutory requirement is not without its critics. There are many both within and beyond the world of education, faith members as well as secularists, politicians and parents, who question the value and appropriateness of what the law demands. In a considerable number of schools, especially secondary, the law is consistently flouted. Practical considerations, such as lack of a space large enough for all the school to gather in, are put forward. On a more philosophical level it is argued that to 'require' children and young people to worship is not only an infringement of their human rights but is counterproductive and certainly does not mean that worship actually takes place. It is not unknown for adults to state as the reason for not attending church that they were 'inoculated against it' at school by 'all those boring assemblies'. A case could certainly be made for ensuring that there are regular, but not necessarily daily, acts of worship. This could help to ensure that such acts are of a high quality, and many schools justify their less than full compliance with the law by just such an argument. A survey of the 2006 SACRE reports indicated that the quality of the experience of collective worship was more important than simply its frequency, and included the view that good worship supports the spiritual development of young people and not merely moral and social development. This is where some secondary schools have failed.

If there are to be regular acts of worship in schools then it is important, from a faith point of view, that they are good and actually provide the opportunity to worship. An assembly of the school community has its own value. Coming together in this way fosters a sense of corporate identity. It can be a time for providing information, for celebrating success, for welcome and farewells. The head teacher referred to at the start of this section did not set out to be 'worshipped' but did have a strong conviction about the importance of the whole school identity and his leadership role within that. He saw the daily assembly as significant to the ethos of the school. He may well have had a point. But adding a hymn and a quick prayer to such an event does not turn it into an act of worship. An assembly where there is also a true piece of collective worship says something significant about the school's ethos.

In a church school the daily act of collective worship can play an important part in reflecting and developing the school's distinctive ethos. What needs to be done to ensure that it offers opportunities for **worship**?

Planning, time and place

There are very few members of the clergy who can preach a good sermon from three words jotted down on a piece of paper. There are very few good acts of collective worship that have not required careful planning. Such planning is much more than simply the preparation for a specific act of worship. It goes back to a school's collective worship policy and the designation of someone to take a lead responsibility. It will most likely entail the choice of a theme for the worship, either on a termly or half-termly basis, and giving advance notice of who will be doing what. This is particularly important if the plan involves outside speakers who can bring their own insights and experience from their personal faith and cultural traditions.

The church school has an advantage here in that it has a ready entrée into the local church and is one of the important links that can be made between school and church (see chapter 9). But while church schools should be true to their trust deeds in this matter, it does not preclude them from inviting members of others denominations and faiths into the school to be involved in acts of worship. Indeed, this should be encouraged. Care, however, needs to be taken that non-Christians are not asked to lead Christian acts of worship.

Decisions about time and place are also significant in the planning of collective worship. There is the temptation to plan the timetable and then fit in collective worship around that. If a church school believes that worship is important, then its place in the school day should be given a higher priority than simply convenience. Local situations of course vary and schools will make their decisions in the light of their local knowledge. But whenever the act of worship occurs in the day it should be given sufficient time.

Sometimes collective worship will be in the large space of the school hall when all of the school is present. At other times it could be in smaller areas such as classrooms or studios, with perhaps just a tutor group present. Church schools are allowed to hold their collective worship in the local church, but the frequency of this will largely depend on practical considerations. Where the church is literally next door to the school, the church might be used daily. In other circumstances, once a term might be more realistic. Whatever the space being used, careful thought needs to be given as to the impact of that space upon worship. What will work well in the intimate environment of the classroom could well be lost in the spaciousness of a church. A glorious and expansive act of seasonal celebration has more scope in the larger setting and could feel cramped if confined to a classroom.

Worship at its best has an element of drama about it, and just as producers and directors give careful consideration to how best to use the space being used in order to obtain the effect looked for, the same kind of care should be taken by those responsible for collective worship. It takes planning. A priest who was responsible for some very major services at a large cathedral was often asked if he was nervous at the start of them. 'No,' he used to say, 'the time for being nervous was when it was all being planned. If I planned it well there's no need to be nervous now.' And what he meant by planning was not just all the obvious administrative issues about who was involved or even the liturgical content of the service. It was what he called the 'choreography', the planning of movement and effect – planned so carefully that it made its impact but in such a way that no one was aware of it. Few teachers are trained liturgists, but through the local church and the diocese it is possible to draw upon the expertise that is available.

Church architects and those responsible for the ordering of the interior space of churches make conscious efforts to ensure that worshippers focus upon what is significant. What is felt to be significant will vary with the theology of the particular church community but in Anglican churches there are normally two clear points of focus: the altar, or Lord's Table, and the pulpit. This reflects a theology that draws together both the sacrament of the Eucharist (the Lord's Supper) and the ministry of the Word. The seating arrangement, the raised setting of altar and pulpit, the presence of colour in reredos or east window, altar frontals and pulpit pall, all help to draw attention to what is important and potent. A school should give similar attention to its worship area by providing a clear focal point that conveys significance. It may not be possible for this to be a permanent focus, but by the skilful use of banners and screens, artefacts and lighting, it is possible to provide a setting for worship that is itself worshipful. Few schools have specially designed worship areas and many have to contend with considerable disadvantages. Governors, staff and pupils will then need to give extra and imaginative thought as to how these can best be overcome.

How far do governors and staff draw upon the liturgical expertise available to them locally and in the diocese to help ensure collective worship is effective, making use of the local church as one possible setting for worship?

Common and distinctive

There are numerous resources for schools to draw on in preparing for collective worship. Dioceses provide help on their websites, and through courses, to assist schools to provide high-quality acts of worship. Church schools do not have a monopoly on good collective worship – indeed, there are community schools where Christians leading worship put some church schools to shame. But there is no excuse for a church school not to deliver good collective worship that is well prepared, creates a sense of worship, has a clear shape to it, uses appropriate language, provides time and space for quiet reflection and prayer, and involves the active participation of the children and young people. Over a period of time there will be different content and emphasis but also a variety of approaches – story and drama, music and mime, description and visual presentation, group involvement and individual leading. Worship will be linked to the life of the school and feed into its life. It will help the exploration of personal belief and diverse beliefs. Time will be given to consider the pupils' needs and the needs of others. There will be celebration and commiseration, times of joy and sorrow, praise and forgiveness. Such worship will offer opportunities for developing an inner sense of God, of what is meant by holiness and the transcendent. It will encourage sensitivity to the views and practices of others. All of this, and no doubt much more, will be common to all good collective worship, whether in a church or community school.

So what then might be distinctive about collective worship in a church school, and specifically in a Church of England school? Local situations will mean that each school has to make decisions about how its Anglican distinctiveness can best and most appropriately be expressed, sensitive to the community it serves.

Liturgical shape

One of the marks of Church of England worship is that it has a clear tradition of liturgy set out initially in the Book of Common Prayer and more recently in *Common Worship*. Although I have known of unwise and educationally unaware clergy who have laid on BCP Matins (Morning Prayer) as a service in church for a primary school, this is certainly not to be recommended. But this does not mean that the insights of this liturgical tradition cannot be drawn on.

At its simplest it means that an act of worship should have a recognisable shape and its elements be liturgically literate. One such shape can be found in *Flippin' Praise*, a worship resource for primary schools produced by CASIAS (Consortium in Anglia for the Statutory Inspection of Anglican Schools) and the Church of England Liturgical Commission. It has a fourfold structure of Gathering, Engaging, Responding and Sending which both relates to many Anglican acts of worship as well as being similar to a familiar format used in school collective worship of welcome, story, song/prayer and dismissal. It is a structure recommended by the Liturgical Commission of the Church of England in its report *Transforming Worship*. Using such a shape creates recognisable links between school and church.

Gathering draws people in as they enter, encouraging them to join in with a song or simply listen quietly to a piece of music. A distinctive atmosphere is created around a clearly visible point of focus. A feeling of expectation should be created.

Engaging is where the main input of the worship occurs, encouraging engagement with the Bible, Christian teaching and God.

Responding offers the opportunity for all, adults and children, to respond in a way that is appropriate for them, providing them with a time to reflect or pray. This is in the spirit of invitation, not compulsion.

Sending relates to leaving an act of worship, which should have purpose and not simply be a physical matter of getting out of the room, and who does so first. This may be marked by singing a song or by a suitable act of ritual, such as extinguishing a candle lit at the beginning of the worship. Both *Gathering* and *Sending* may be accompanied with words from the liturgical tradition such as 'The Lord be with you' and its response 'And with your spirit', or a closing blessing. There should be a sense that children are being 'sent out' in the power of God's Spirit who is always with them.

A church school should ensure that its acts of worship have an appropriate shape, reflective of the Church's tradition of liturgical worship.

The Bible

Part of the Anglican liturgical tradition is the use of a lectionary – a pattern of sequential readings from both the Old and New Testaments in an annual or three-year cycle. It not only provides a degree of continuity (for regular worshippers at least) but also helps to ensure that other passages, besides the vicar's favourites, get read! Church schools should give careful thought to the amount of biblical material used in their worship. One head teacher realised that rather too much time in collective worship had been spent on other faiths when a pupil informed her that Jesus went around with '12 bicycles'. The next term was spent concentrating on stories about Jesus and his disciples. Biblical material is rich in stories that not only relate events but raise issues of serious religious and moral concern, and church secondary schools should give full weight to this aspect of their distinctive heritage.

Two powerful methods of presenting biblical material are *Open the Book* and *Godly Play* (also known as Reflective Story Telling).

The former, which uses dramatised versions of biblical stories, has proved to be a significant means of creating links between schools and their local churches, church members, often in ecumenical teams, providing the set of presenters. *Godly Play*, which originated in the United States, is more suitable for use with smaller groups and provides opportunities for pupils to reflect on different aspects of the biblical story through simple 'I wonder . . .' questions, and art or craft activities.

Seasons

The Church of England, in common with a number of other denominations, follows the Church's year in its worship, celebrating the major festivals such as Christmas and Easter, as well as events from Christian history and the lives of the saints. The seasons are marked by use of the various liturgical colours – white for celebration (e.g. Christmas), red for the saints and the Holy Spirit (e.g. Pentecost), purple for penitence (e.g. Advent and Lent). Alongside this visual reminder of liturgical colours, the seasons and festivals should be reflected in the choice of prayers, symbols and songs. All this gives a particular shape to the year, and provides a link between the worship of the school and the pattern of worship in churches, helping to convey the fact that collective worship is connected with and part of a global expression of worship throughout the worldwide Church. This connection can be given more obvious expression through links made with schools or churches in other parts of the world where the worship tradition might be very different but, through its diversity, can enrich local forms of worship. Such diversity is a treasure of the Anglican tradition.

The Eucharist

The Eucharist (Holy Communion, Lord's Supper, Mass) is at the heart of worship for many church people, and a church school should at the very least consider whether or not it would be appropriate to hold a Eucharist as either a regular or occasional act of worship. Churches have differing disciplines about the age at which children should receive the consecrated bread and wine, and whether this can be before or only after Confirmation. While this will need to be taken into account by the head teacher and governors this does not in itself prevent there being a school Eucharist. As in other settings it is possible for those who have not been confirmed or who do not normally receive the sacrament, to be welcomed to the altar/Holy Table, for a blessing. This helps to ensure that no one feels excluded even though not all or even many will receive the bread and wine. Careful teaching about the nature of the service and its various and differing aspects such as praise and confession, intercession and the sharing of the peace will be important to make the service an inclusive experience. Most importantly, pupils should learn about what events are being remembered in this service and how what is done relates to the life of Jesus and the Church.

The form of the Eucharist will need careful thought and, especially on the first occasion, to be carefully prepared for, so that those taking part know the significance of its ritual and symbolism, and the whole school community is drawn into this act of thanksgiving (the meaning of the word Eucharist). The service recalls and draws upon the gift of Christ to his people through his death and resurrection, but – in the words of *Common Worship* – it is also the offering of 'ourselves, our souls and bodies', all that we are and all we do. Teaching about the Eucharist should be included in RE but also draw upon other areas of the curriculum – such as art, drama, literacy, history.

Local situations will help determine where the service takes place – in school or in church – and the form of the service may well be influenced by the particular tradition of the local church. Certainly there should be discussion between the priest and the school before a Eucharist is even contemplated. All aspects of the service should receive careful preparation so that it is a good-quality act of worship honouring to God as well as nurturing those present. Too often, worship can centre almost exclusively on the worshippers rather than on the God who is being worshipped. There should also be regular reviews of the way the service is conducted and the impact it is having both on pupils individually and on the school community as a whole.

Where the head teacher and governors decide that it is not appropriate in their situation to hold a school Eucharist, they should ensure that pupils have the opportunity to learn about this central act of worship in the life of the Church. Looking at the Eucharist makes a good whole school topic or theme day.

Worship is central to the life of a church and it is central to what is distinctive about a church school. Staff and governors of church schools will wish to give it a high priority when considering how the school can offer a distinctive experience to the children and young people for whom they are responsible.

Intangibles

There is an intangible element to this distinctiveness – an element that is not to be found in what is done or said, in the forms that are used or the schemes followed. It is that which grows out of the life of a community where faith is held and lived by. It is, as it were, the spirit of worship that a community of faith shares, grows by. It is what both reflects and shapes the Christian ethos of that community. It may be quite tentative, or vigorous and strong. But it exists in a church school (or should) in a way that it seldom does, if ever, in a community school. Intangible but real, it is the product of the outworking of much of what this book has been about. To put it in religious terms, it is the presence of the Spirit of God in a place where a community of faith is itself open to the working of that Spirit. It is why, in the end, distinctiveness is not just a collection of neatly phrased policies or value statements on the wall – helpful as these might be – but is to do with the 'lived-outness' of faith treasured and committed to.

Those who say that you can tell there is something distinctive about a church school as soon as you enter it are bearing witness to this. But it does not happen by chance or without thought, imagination, prayer and discipline. It is a kind of holiness – although I am sure many staff and governors would be surprised by such a word – that grows out of search as well as discovery, of question as well as answer, of doubt as well as affirmation. The distinctiveness of a church school is open-ended without being wishy-washy, inclusive without denying its very foundations in the Christian story. It looks for the reality of God from the reality of what it is to be human. It is not some cosy, pious escapism from the ambiguity of our lives and complexity of what it is to be growing and developing as children and young people and as the community committed to them. It is a mystery, and that is why it is in worship that one comes closest to it.

More than
Caring and
Sharing

NINE

School, church and community

Asked what he felt was most distinctive about his church school one head teacher said that it was the connection with the local church. He valued the relationship that had been built up with the vicar, who frequently visited the school and was on the governing body. Services were regularly held in church and a number of the local congregation helped in various ways in the school. During a recent inspection the pupils, on their own initiative, had asked the inspector to visit 'our church'. There was a very positive and mutual relationship between school and church. The head's own experience had not always been in church schools and he saw this as something that set them apart from community schools.

While this would be true of many church schools it is not universally so. There are clergy who do not see the value of making close links with schools in their parishes. Others have no aptitude for what they call 'work with children', and so avoid schools. There are PCCs that never have items about their school on the agenda and churches that do not welcome children and young people into the building. The lost opportunities are immense and this at a time when congregations bewail the lack of contact with the younger generation. Much is said about the need to be open to young people and children, to organise services that are accessible for them or organised by the young people themselves, but for all the talk the reality shows that the Church is losing out on yet another generation. If there is to be mission to and among children and young people the most obvious place for this to be realised is in and through schools. Little wonder that Lord Dearing's report said that church schools are at the centre of the Church's mission. This is not about proselytising. It is about the offering of a distinctive approach to the development of young people through the education system. It is about serving them in ways that relate to their humanity in all its fullness. It is about keeping the story of Christianity alive as a possibility for their own faith position.

In the appointment of parish clergy, dioceses, patrons and parishes need to give very careful consideration to the significance and needs of local schools as one of their mission priorities.

The clergy

In the 1960s a book called *God's Frozen People* by Ian Gibbs and T. Ralph Morton drew attention to the position of lay people in the Church, the fact that they were largely, albeit benignly, dominated by the clergy and were given comparatively little opportunity to make positive contributions to the life of the Church, especially at the points of real decision making. There were always the 'flower ladies' and church cleaners, but the attitude that 'Father knows best' was commonplace, maintained by a mutual collusion. The rediscovery of the place of the laity in the life, ministry and mission of the Church has been a cultural change and has released the gifts of lay people in ways that fifty years ago would have seemed impossible. These days the clergy share their ministry not only with other accredited ministers such as Readers but with various ministry teams of lay people. Collaborative ministry is the expected pattern and has revitalised the Church in many places. But not all.

Many clergy have welcomed this, some have resisted, some have found that despite their efforts to involve lay people in ministry and mission there has been little response. The picture is mixed, and generalisations are difficult and probably not very helpful. But it is clear that over the last fifty years the role of the clergy has changed, not least because there are less of them (in all denominations) and, in rural areas especially, this has meant that more and more parishes have been brought together under the leadership of one full-time paid vicar. Priorities have had to change and styles of working have tended to become more managerial. But the leadership role remains, even if it has had to be understood in new ways. Ordained men and women are rightly expected to be leaders with a significant representative role. In an increasingly secularised and multi-cultural society this role will be different from the past and no doubt considerably diminished but it is not lost, neither within congregations nor within the wider community. It is most dramatically seen in times of community tragedy and at annual Remembrance Services held in churches and at war memorials. But the leadership and representative role is also seen in the more everyday life of a community – and not least in relation to its schools.

While there are some clergy who resist attempts to involve them in their local church school, it is also true that some schools are less than welcoming to the local clergy. There may have been bad experiences in the past. But for a church school whose ethos should include forgiveness and reconciliation, the harbouring of past hurts or failings does not set a good example. Some clergy are nervous about being involved with children or young people. Some will be excellent with teenagers but terrified of infants. And the opposite can be true. Where there is anxiety or lack of experience the school itself can help the clergy, and clergy should be open to such help. Clergy do not have to lead school worship if that is not their gift but they can still be present as a sign of their care for the school. Ordination training by courses or colleges can seldom give enough time to train those with no experience or aptitude for leading collective worship and not every curate has the opportunity to go into schools. Dioceses, through their Continuing Ministerial Education programme, can make a difference but the real help is always most effective in the locality and 'on the job'. Where it is not possible (or desirable) for the local ordained person to be either a governor or regular visitor to a school, other accredited ministers should be sought.

SACREs and Diocesan Boards of Education can help by offering, both to schools and to visitors, some simple protocols and guidelines that not only clarify the position on safeguarding issues but set out what the school can expect of the visitor and what the visitor can expect of the school. Visitors who are going to lead or be involved in collective worship need to know if there is a theme being followed and what other work in the school might relate to what occurs in 'assembly'. There should be discussion between the clergy and the head, or person responsible for collective worship, helping to ensure that what is proposed is both generally suitable and appropriate for the range of age groups present. Feedback from both staff and children can be most helpful. Not only children must be willing to learn!

Clergy are, as it were, the 'official face' of the Church. They can be the focus of fantasies and fears, of false expectations and unrealistic demands. It is valuable both to the Church and to a community for children to grow up neither overawed nor ignorant of clergy. It is incumbent upon clergy to make the very best use of the opportunities that visiting a school can offer. It is of course more than a simple PR exercise, but there is an element of that to it and thought needs to be given to what impression of the Church and of the Christian faith its representative is giving.

Clergy are not simply worship leaders, and much of their role will be of a more pastoral nature. As regular visitors to a school, clergy have the opportunity to establish a good relation with the head and other staff. Head teachers in particular can find themselves in a demanding and quite lonely position, and a ready and understanding listening ear can be very valuable. Some skill is required, however, when the local vicar is also a foundation governor (as is common), and especially when he/she is chair of governors. The governors have a managerial role that is increasingly scrutinised and complex, including that of being a 'friendly critic', or 'critical friend', requiring the ability to show both caring understanding and a degree of objectivity. Clergy generally have a default pastoral mode, which, of course, is very valuable but needs to be set within the specific role they have in the school. This can be of particular importance when there are issues of discipline or capability among staff and where the governors not only have a responsibility to care for staff but are also their employers (as in aided schools), while retaining a primary responsibility for the well-being and good education of the pupils and students.

The presence of the local vicar at school events can be a form of tokenism, but where the relations between church and school are good it can be very significant, emphasising the church link but also giving reality to the title of the school as a church school.

The ordained person, as a foundation governor, has both an opportunity and responsibility to help the governing body and the school to articulate its Christian ethos and the theological basis for its distinctiveness.

The laity

For the world in general there are only two kinds of clergy in the Church of England: bishops and vicars. All the distinctions of full-time or part-time, stipendiary or self-supporting, priests and deacons, canons and archdeacons, rural deans and cathedral deans usually have little meaning outside church circles. Clergy are the Church's professionals and, for good or ill, that fact inevitably sets them apart. As I have been told more than once when explaining a Christian viewpoint, 'Well, you would say that, it's your job!' But this is not true of the laity, and it gives them a powerful and important position when it comes to living and speaking about the faith.

As we have seen in the chapter on RE, the national guidelines expect the learning experience in RE to consider what faiths are about and what those who live by a faith have to say about its impact on their lives and behaviour. Members of the local church(es) can make a significant contribution to the school experience of what Christianity means. Often their voice is even more telling than that of the clergy in this respect, especially if they are able to relate their faith to their work and to issues and moral questions that arise in the place of employment.

Church schools should look for suitable lay people from their local church who are willing and able to speak about their faith in the context of either collective worship or an RE lesson.

Open the Book is a powerful way in which local church people, working in teams, can present biblical material in dramatised form to young people. The team itself learns from the experience and often involves lay people who are prepared to work as part of a group but who would be unwilling to do the same kind of thing on their own. Young people enjoy and value the way the Bible stories are presented, and that is enhanced when the stories are related to other areas of learning and go beyond the act of collective worship.

Schools increasingly welcome and value the contribution that visiting adults can make to the life of the school – both in terms of the curriculum and in terms of social understanding and development. Helping youngsters with their reading is not the only thing visitors can do – valuable as that may be. Local people may well have skills and abilities that bring additional support to the work of the school, whether that be in areas of art and music, or practical and technical skills. Parish musicians, for example, might well share their expertise in supporting music in school worship and more generally.

The importance of informed, committed and concerned governors can hardly be overstated. Foundation governors provide an important link between the school and the parish, and the appointment of a governor should be seen as a significant piece of Christian ministry. Governors should be valued and supported by the church community and the PCC, and there should be a culture of affirmation towards all who are involved in education. Just as parishes should consider the way in which they can encourage the vocation to the priestly ministry, thought should also be given to how vocations to the teaching profession might be encouraged and supported.

Links between the school, the local church and the community will normally depend for their development and long-term sustainability on the efforts of lay people, whether or not the original initiative came from the clergy. Such links may be focused on one-off events, on annual ventures such as a spring fair or holiday play scheme, or on more regular activities as part of the Extended School programme. Many schools run lunch or tea clubs for the elderly at which children not only act as hosts but also help in the preparation of the food and in serving those who attend. Such interrelated events play their part in helping a school become aware of the Christian community engaged in a range of activities – not just religious – but it also makes for social cohesion, especially where the community events have an ecumenical or inter-faith element.

Christians in both the school and the Church need to be imaginative and open to the contribution and involvement of all members of the local community when considering ways in which they can add to the learning and social experience of pupils and students, and serve the community.

It is not just links locally that are important. The life of the county or region in which the school is set will have its impact on the young people, not least through its landscape, local industries and commerce, employment and leisure opportunities. Schools are sometimes rightly criticised for being good at making local and global links while failing to develop regional links and understanding. This can be equally true with regard to the Church. Church schools may well have very good links with their local church and with a community in another part of the world yet be unaware of the diversity of church life within a diocese and of the resources that are available through a diocesan link. The family of church schools in a diocese can be a valuable and helpful network, helping to establish links between heads and staff, governors and clergy, parents and diocesan officers.

Church and school

The church/school link is not only a matter of the connections that individuals make – important as they are. There are, as it were, institutional links – things that a school and church each do as part of their corporate life, reflecting that the school has a Christian foundation and the parish has a concern for its church school.

The most obvious, yet often neglected, of these is prayer. Whatever else prayer is, it includes the notion of attentive concern, a conscious expression of the desire for another's well-being. In Christian understanding it rings rather hollow if a person – or an institution

– talks about a concern for someone but never includes that person or group in their prayers. Church and school should each regularly include prayers for one another, their life and members. Special events – the arrival of a new incumbent, an Ofsted inspection, a school trip, the visit of a bishop – should be included in the prayers of school and church. This, of course, means that each knows what is occurring and is of particular significance for the other. Good communication is important. Prayer needs to be informed. School news-sheets and parish magazines provide opportunities for the mutual sharing of information.

The creation of a prayer group that welcomes members from both the school and the church has proved to be very significant in the life of many churches and schools. Experience shows that what begins as a concern for each other widens into a concern for other schools and for wider church and community life. This then underpins a school's action and service, locally and in the wider world. Through the Anglican Communion a school can tap into a global organisation within which specific links can be forged, providing an interchange of information, personal communication and giving.

While many churches continue to hold Sunday schools or their equivalent in the context of or alongside Sunday worship, there are many others for whom this is no longer a realistic proposition. Some have taken the opportunity to establish a group that meets out of school time but in the church school, providing not only input on the Christian faith and a time of worship but also games and other activities. Although this may be led by the local clergy it most often involves lay members of the local church.

Just as foundation governors have a responsibility to help the school community understand and develop the implications of its Christian foundation, so too the local church should be informed about its local church school. Church notice-boards should include information about the school – and be kept up to date. Exhibitions of school work in the church are both informative and decorative. They draw the attention of congregations to the fact that there is a church school locally and to something of what it does. The level of ignorance on such matters in some places is saddening and speaks loudly of lost opportunities.

If it is important that foundation governors should occasionally ask, 'When did the governing body last consider its mission statement?' It is equally important that a Parish Church Council should consider when it last had the church school on its agenda and whether the school features in its mission statement.

Much is made in a parish of when a new incumbent is instituted or licensed. There is a big service, for which the church is usually crowded, as people come to welcome them and see what they are like. Representatives of local organisations, local politicians and local churches are not only usually present but are typically given the opportunity in the service to welcome the new priest. It is important that any head teacher and chair of governors in the benefice is also invited and takes part. This speaks significantly of the link between church and school. But if that link is really to have proper and mutual meaning should not a church also mark the arrival of a new head, arranging a service that specifically welcomes and prays for them?

Church schools make varied use of the local church for acts of worship. For large schools it may not be possible to accommodate the whole school in the local church at any one time, and arrangements have to take this into account. But most churches are certainly large enough and should be pleased to welcome the school into its building for worship. When the distance between church and school is short, this may well be possible on a regular basis. When distances are greater, it will be more difficult, and a termly service, based on a major festival, may be the best arrangement. Education Sunday offers a particularly suitable occasion for a service when church and school can come together. Suitable resource material for this service is circulated to parishes every year by the National Society and is available on their website (http://www.natsoc.org.uk/).

As we have discussed in the last chapter, the setting of worship within a church building is significant, but simply opening the church for use by the school does not exhaust the opportunities this can offer in terms of developing the relationship between the two. Involvement of local church members in making the school feel welcome, offering refreshments and having a part in the worship enhances the experience and the link between church and school. So too does occasionally welcoming the school to the regular worship of the church and giving the children an active part there in the service. It is helpful to have a number of prayers and hymns/songs that are known both by the school and the church for such occasions. There does need to be clarity, however, when church and school are involved together in worship, not least in sorting out who makes what arrangements. It can be useful to ask the simple question: is this a school service involving the church or a church service involving the school?

Churches are a resource for more than just acts of worship. They are a rich treasure house for all aspects of the curriculum. This is obviously true of history and sociology, for example, but there is much that a church can offer to the teaching of mathematics in terms of space and shape and calculation. The artefacts, vestments and stained glass windows not only tell stories and demonstrate the use of symbolism but are an inspiration for art and writing. Church records are primary documents for local history and are examples of different written formats, from report to official record, minutes to accounts. It is important that a visit to a church is not simply a matter of listing what is in it but that each item, be it pulpit or font, reredos or rood screen, is understood in terms of its purpose and meaning and the way it relates to the Christian faith. As places of prayer, churches offer spaces for quiet and reflection. The churchyard, too, is rich in learning opportunities – as an introduction to large questions around death and memory, but also to matters of conservation, ecology and wild areas.

The link between a church and its local school should be a rich and mutual relationship enhancing the life of each and developing the distinctive ethos of the school.

TEN

Statutory Inspection of Anglican schools (SIAS)

One very obvious distinctive element in the life of a church school is that it receives an inspection in addition to that of Ofsted, usually about four weeks later. This is variously known as the Denominational inspection, the Church inspection, a Section 48 inspection (with reference to the 2005 Education Act) or, for Church of England schools, SIAS (Statutory Inspection of Anglican Schools). As the latter title indicates, this is not a voluntary inspection but one required by law. It replaced the previous Section 23 inspections. The format and process of the inspection was agreed in discussions between the Department of Science and Education and the National Society, the latter being the accrediting body for SIAS inspectors and responsible for the training of inspectors and monitoring of inspections. Inspection arrangements are organised locally between the church schools and the Diocesan Board of Education. It is the governors who 'employ' the inspector, although payment is made by the National Society from a government grant.

'The Framework for Inspection and Self-evaluation of Church of England Schools' (National Society, 2005, p. 2), quoting from the *The Way Ahead* (p. 2), makes it clear that the inspection framework 'provides a process for evaluating the extent to which church schools are *"distinctively and recognizably Christian institutions"*'.

The inspections are not primarily descriptions of what the distinctive elements are but an evaluation of them and their effectiveness. The Framework again quotes from *The Way Ahead* report: '*with the State being a willing provider of education, the justification for the Church's presence in education must be to offer an approach to education which is distinctively Christian*'. It goes on: 'A Church of England school's self-evaluation, *verified by inspection*, will seek to judge how well the school's distinctive Christian character and values ensure the development and achievement of the *whole* child or young person' (p. 6, quoting *The Way Ahead*, p. 19).

As the body responsible for SIAS inspections, the National Society undertakes careful monitoring of the whole inspection process and seeks to ensure consistency among inspectors, who not only receive initial training but are required to undertake annual ongoing professional development. The latest information available (December 2010) indicates that a more rigorous process is being adopted, with particular emphasis upon assessment criteria and additional training to develop skills for making secure judgements in RE. The training programme is designed to ensure that there is an improved level of inspector competency at the point of accreditation. This is of particular significance, because a distinctive feature of SIAS inspections is that inspectors operate as a solo inspector, which means there is little opportunity once initial training has been completed for the observation of good practice by colleagues.

Self-evaluation

The Framework makes it clear that a vital element in the process is self-evaluation. Schools had become used to a process of self-evaluation formalised in the Ofsted requirement that they complete a Self-Evaluation Form (SEF). Church schools were encouraged to complete an additional SIAS SEF, although this was not mandatory.

Head teachers, staff and governors are well aware of the time and effort involved in completing such forms, and may have been relieved when the government decided in 2010 that SEFs would no longer be required, but the fact remains that self-evaluation in one guise or another is still going to be necessary. Self-evaluation is not simply an exercise to satisfy inspectors but is a necessary part of a school's self-monitoring programme. Irksome though it may sometimes seem, the process of consciously reflecting on what is going on in the school and articulating where there are strengths and where there are areas needing development is important. The SEF was a prompt to some schools to make sure they carried out this piece of monitoring. When done, it should be made available to the inspector prior to the inspection.

Some church school head teachers felt that the requirement of a separate SEF for the SIAS inspection was a step too far and made the choice not to complete one. They argued that much of the material was already in the Ofsted SEF and time could be better spent on other things. It was their choice, although they were probably the losers, not least because the absence of a Self-Evaluation Form made the task of the inspector that bit more difficult and more dependent on what was observed on a particular day rather than drawing upon a school's longer term overview of how it saw itself. Those who did complete the SEF often found it to be a demanding piece of work requiring them to articulate, *with evidence*, both what was distinctively Christian about their school and the effectiveness of this. Demanding but worth it.

The temptation is to see the SEF as a piece of work produced purely to satisfy the inspection, after which it can then be put away till the next time. This defeats half the value of the SEF, which is intended to be a continuing working document acting as a check against which to test ongoing improvement and action.

Governors should review the SIAS SEF on a regular basis, relating it to the overall School Development Plan and School Improvement Plan and ensuring that it is kept up to date. Not to do so is a sign that distinctiveness is not considered to be important even though it constitutes the primary justification for the existence of a church school.

Assistance in preparing for the SIAS inspection is offered both by the National Society, through downloads on its website, and by the local Diocesan Board of Education. A toolkit is available from the National Society to assist schools in the completion of the SEF. This is a thorough and extensive document which some have found rather daunting; some diocesan education boards, as a result, rather than providing a lengthy catalogue of provision, have offered a more simplified version that concentrates on the key questions looked at during an inspection (see, for example, www.ChurchschoolsEast. org.uk).

Effectiveness

The key focus of the whole process is on the *effect* that the Christian ethos of the church school has on *the learner*. Clearly that implies that the school (and the inspector) knows what a Christian ethos looks like when they see it and the ways it can have a positive effect upon pupils and students. It may be something that is felt – an atmosphere, a characteristic way in which staff and pupils relate to each other – but simply to state that this exists and that people know it when they see it will not be enough. Evidence is required, and judgement about its effectiveness needs to be made in terms of each particular school, not according to some preconceived understanding of what makes for a distinctive effectiveness.

In gathering evidence an inspector can be expected to look at school documents, e.g. the SEF and policy documents on subjects like RE, collective worship, social cohesion, behaviour, etc., but the existence of documents does not itself guarantee effectiveness. So inspectors will visit classrooms and, in voluntary aided schools, observe RE lessons. They will also attend an act of collective worship, and will want to talk with staff, with pupils and students, with foundation governors and, where possible, with parents and representatives of the local church. They will consider the school environment, assessing how far displays and artefacts support the message that this is a church school. The views of learners will be very significant in all this.

Four key questions

The inspection, and therefore the SEF, concentrates upon four key questions:

- How well does the school, through its distinctive Christian character, meet the needs of all learners?
- What is the impact of collective worship on the school community?
- How effective is the religious education? (VA schools only.)
- How effective are the leadership and management of the school as a church school?

The needs of all learners

A church school, in common with community schools, should always endeavour to ensure that the needs of each pupil or student are being met and that all feel valued. But this is easier to state than to put into consistent practice. Various pressures, both upon the school as a whole and on a particular teacher, can result in certain groups of children being given less attention than they need, be they

SEN children, 'middle' achievers, travellers' children, the gifted and able, or those for whom English is not their first language. This may not be intentional or even conscious. It may be a temporary matter arising from a recent piece of internal monitoring or an Ofsted visit. A teacher may be having difficulties with appropriate differentiation in provision and assessment. A school may have identified a weakness across a curriculum area, such as writing or problem solving, or in general performance at a particular Key Stage. The temptation is to improve its position in achievement tables by concentrating on where the weakness lies and taking attention away from other areas. This will mean that some children will not be receiving what they need. Academic achievement may be considered so important that less attention is given to social education. Most children may cope quite happily with this; others will feel that their needs are not being met. It is therefore very important that a school and each of its teachers work positively to ensure that there is a consistent effort to meet the needs of every pupil and student.

The Framework highlights respect, justice and equality as aspects of the Christian ethos and values of the school through which pupils feel secure, happy and confident, valued and special. Inspectors look for evidence from pupils that they find their work both enjoyable and meaningful. As noted in earlier chapters, such concepts are not uniquely Christian, but through the inspector's discussions with pupils, staff and governors the underlying distinctively Christian ethos should become clear.

In personal development and relations with others, both peers and adults, pupils will be expected to show personal responsibility, compassion and hope, spiritual self-awareness, independence, and a readiness to support others, sensitive to their needs and views. Relationships across the school community will be collaborative and mutually supportive, with conflict dealt with compassionately and fairly, in a spirit of forgiveness and reconciliation. The school environment will be expected to have a very positive impact upon the quality of spiritual reflection, prayer and worship, and to include displays that support RE as well as general learning.

The impact of collective worship

The legal requirement that there should be collective worship of a mainly Christian form available to all pupils and students to the age of 16 has been a contentious issue ever since the 1944 Education Act. Pressure has been placed upon successive governments to make changes to this requirement but to no effect. Not all schools, especially secondary ones, comply with the full letter of the law. But this should not be the case in church schools and SIAS inspectors will indicate whether a school is meeting the statutory requirements or not.

Church schools are expected to do much more than simply meet the legal requirements. Inspectors want to see not only evidence that there are regular acts of collective worship but, more significantly, that these have a positive impact upon the whole life of the school community and on its witness to the community beyond the school. The acts of worship themselves should be well planned, imaginative and inspiring, ensuring learner participation. Responses from all who attend should be positive. While collective worship should be clearly Christian, in Church of England schools drawing especially upon the resources of the Anglican tradition from across the world, it should also be sensitive to the different cultural and faith backgrounds of all pupils and students. Each should find the worship supportive of their spiritual development. Elements from across the curriculum should be drawn upon in the worship, which in turn should impact upon various areas of the curriculum. There should be evidence of good relations with the local church, parish and clergy. Where there are celebrations of the Eucharist, inspectors will want to see how far learners are involved and how they respond to the experience. It is reasonable to expect students from a church school to know the Lord's Prayer by heart and to be aware of the seasons and major festivals in the Church's calendar. The level of staff attendance at and involvement in the acts of worship is one of the clear indicators of how seriously a school takes collective worship.

Foundation governors should take an active interest in the collective worship of their school, ensuring that a clear record is kept of the programme of worship and monitoring its impact within the whole life of the school.

Religious Education

It is only in voluntary aided schools that RE is directly inspected by the SIAS inspectors. It is assumed that Ofsted inspections will look at this aspect of the curriculum in voluntary controlled schools – but that does not always happen. If a voluntary controlled school specifically wishes to have its RE inspected then this would need to be arranged with the inspector and there could be a charge, as it goes beyond the contractual requirements.

As an area of the curriculum, RE can be assessed in terms of the levels of achievement that pupils and students attain, in relation both to their age and to their achievement in other subjects. As a subject, RE has its own discipline, and calls upon learning skills that both relate to other curriculum areas and integrate them in a creative way – e.g. literature, philosophy, history, cultural studies, ethics, etc. In recent years there has been an increase in taking RE to examination level and it is very disappointing to find church aided secondary schools where there is no public examination in RE. It undermines other efforts to ensure that RE is taken seriously and is effective. The absence of an RE specialist, the use of TAs as subject coordinators, and less than 5 per cent of curriculum time being given to RE, can further indicate that a school lacks confidence and conviction in marking its Christian distinctiveness.

The SIAS inspector looks for the same level of planning, subject knowledge, imaginative presentation and monitoring in RE as would be looked for in any curriculum subject. Pupils and students should be able to explain how the subject impacts on their lives, and all RE teaching should aspire to be inspiring and relevant to the needs of the learners. One of the things that is often said about church schools is that they are places where talk about God is not only possible but encouraged and readily engaged in – no matter the differing faith and belief positions held within the school community. Its significance in both moral and spiritual development is understood. Such discussion must, of course, be open in nature and, while critically aware, not judgemental. The RE syllabus, whether a locally agreed or diocesan syllabus, will give a major place to the study of the Christian faith, but all students are required to study other religions and inspectors test to see that this is the case. A Church of England school should include understanding drawn from a specifically Anglican tradition, but in many cases this is done with less confidence than in teaching about Christianity in general.

A church school expresses the seriousness with which it views RE by such indicators as the resourcing of RE in teacher time and learning resources, the careful monitoring of RE, and the overall attainment levels of its pupils. Foundation governors should have a special concern for such matters.

Leadership and management

SIAS inspections have always looked for evidence of the effectiveness of the foundation governors and head teacher in the leadership and management of the school as they promote its Christian vision. Together with the increased emphasis in Ofsted inspections on the role of governors in the management of the school, this means that governors can expect a thorough examination of their role. Some view this as yet another pressure upon them in addition to the increasing demands on their time and commitment. While it is repeatedly emphasised that they are not expected to make professional educational decisions, the fact remains that many governors see their responsibilities as increasingly technical in nature and complex in character. It is to the credit of governors that so many undertake this responsibility with great commitment and skill. It can, however, be difficult to find good governors, not least in small communities. Christian congregations should take governorship seriously as a significant piece of Christian service and an expression of Christian ministry and witness.

Foundation governors have a key role in shaping the vision statement of their school. While help can be obtained from national or diocesan examples of vision statements, it is important that governing bodies make such statements their own. Statements that do not include reference to the Christian faith and its values will not be distinctive. But vision statements on their own, especially those that are very general in character, do not achieve much, hence the emphasis placed in this book upon spelling out the distinctive nature of the core Christian values.

In what ways are foundation governors involved in the creation and review of your school's distinctive vision statement?

Inspectors look for evidence from their discussion with pupils, parents and community members that the vision is having an impact on the school and is publicly known, both through the way members of the school community relate to each other and through the school's relationship with the wider community. They will also look for evidence in such documents as the school's prospectus. While it will usually be the head teacher who most obviously articulates the school's vision, foundation governors are expected to support the head teacher in this and see that the school reflects the aims of the school's trust deed. Strong and effective pastoral, practical and spiritual links between the school and parish help to support the school in promoting its Christian vision.

As well as being supportive of the head teacher and whole school community in developing and promoting the school's distinctive Christian character, foundation governors are expected to ensure that there are effective monitoring processes in place to ensure an effective self-evaluation of the school *as a church school*. This will, on occasions, lead quite properly to their challenging the school's leadership, not least in improving standards in RE and collective worship.

Foundation governors and staff in a church school need to have a clear and articulated understanding of the Christian values that shape the school's distinctive vision and that form the basis for its self-evaluation and improvement as a church school.

It seldom happens that all staff members in a Church of England school are Anglican, or indeed Christian, however desirable this might be. Even in Roman Catholic schools the ideal is not always attainable. It is not necessarily just making a virtue of necessity when church schools speak positively of having staff from differing denominational backgrounds or belief positions. What is important, however, is the degree to which the whole staff team is committed to the ethos and vision of the school. One of the responsibilities placed upon head teachers and foundation governors is that of ensuring that all staff are aware of and feel they have a place in developing that ethos and vision. Opportunities should be given for all staff to benefit from training, discussion and reflection on the various aspects of what it means to be a church school.

Throughout this book the emphasis upon what is distinctive has been seen in tandem with the necessity that the church school is a fully inclusive community. This should also be reflected in the school's self-evaluation and in its actions to bring about improvement. Governors and senior leadership teams have particular responsibilities for this, but inspectors also look to see how learners and parents/carers are involved in that process. Conscious effort needs to be made to ensure that this happens on a regular basis so that the views of pupils and parents are not only sought but valued and taken note of.

The distinctiveness of a church school should be supported by and supportive of its local church and community. Inspectors look for evidence of these links and the impact they have. Involvement of members of the local community can be highly beneficial to the learners in the school in widening their experience and developing their skills. But the school community also has much to offer its local community both as a place of meeting and in offering it service. This should be high on the agenda of a church school, one of whose values should be the service of others, corporately as well as individually. At one level, as mentioned earlier, this may involve youngsters in hosting and running lunches for the elderly; at another, it might revolve around a partnership between the school and local businesses.

Beyond the inspection

The departure of the inspector and receipt of a reasonable report may produce a sigh of relief on the part of staff and governors, but even very good reports will usually include some suggested areas for development and it is important that these are taken seriously and acted upon. Actions should be included in the School Improvement Plan and its development plan. There may well be points that involve modification of the school environment, and the buildings sub-committee will need to take this into their Building Development Plan.

Just as the SEF should have been the product of discussion, not least between the head teacher and foundation governors, so too should future action. In responding to a point made in a report it is possible to take decisions that meet the letter of what's said but not really the underlying intention. At one school, the report stated that the inspector would like to see more evidence of its Christian character. The head decided, without consulting the foundation governors, that what was needed was a large Bible visible in the entrance area. The one she obtained was certainly visible. It was large, in fine leather binding and had probably been used as a lectern Bible in a church. It was, however, traditional in language (the King James version) and had Victorian engravings for illustrations. The message it gave out was not what the inspector had had in mind.

If a school should go into Special Measures or be put on Notice to Improve this does not necessarily mean that the SIAS report also views the school as altogether inadequate. There would be something very odd if such a school had an outstanding judgement from SIAS but there may well be strengths in its Christian character despite other weaknesses. In making the concentrated effort necessary for such a school to improve, it is possible to forget the aspects that relate to its distinctiveness as a church school and that could provide some of the strengths it needs to build on. The staff and governors need to remain aware of this and act accordingly.

Church school governors and staff should have confidence in the positive value of the distinctive Christian character of their school, not least when the school goes through a difficult time as the result of inspection visits.

Categories of church schools – the differences

	Voluntary aided	Voluntary controlled	Foundation
Buildings	Owned by trustees. Trust deed determines basis on which school is run. Capital building work is responsibility of governors (supported by government grants of up to 90 per cent of approved expenditure). Playing fields provided by LA.	Owned by trustees. Trust deed determines how school shall be run where law does not make this clear. All building works funded by government and LA.	Owned by trustees. Trust deed determines basis on which the school shall be run where law is silent. Playing fields owned by governors All building works funded by government and LA.
Staff – teaching	Employed by governors, paid by LA. Governors may seek evidence of Christian commitment from applicants for teaching posts.	Appointed by governors, employed and paid by LA. Governors bound by LA appointing policies. Governors may satisfy themselves that a candidate for post of head teacher is suitable to support and develop ethos of the school.	Employed by governors, paid by LA. Governors bound by LA appointing policies. Governors may satisfy themselves that a candidate for post of head teacher is suitable to support and develop ethos of the school.

	Voluntary aided	Voluntary controlled	Foundation
Staff – support	Employed either by governors or contractors. If employed by governors they are paid by LA.	Employed either by LA or contractors. LA employees usually appointed by governors. Paid by the LA.	Employed either by governors or contractors. If employed by governors they are paid by LA
Worship	Reflects Anglican tradition and can include worship in the parish church.	Reflects Anglican tradition and can include worship in the parish church.	Reflects Anglican tradition and can include worship in the parish church.
RE	Governors determine a syllabus that reflects the Anglican tradition. May use a diocesan syllabus where this exists. National Society produced guidance on following an LA syllabus based on National RE Framework with additions set out in their *Excellence and Distinctiveness* report.	School must follow the LA Agreed Syllabus unless the parents request a denominational one. Foundation governors have rights in the appointment of staff (called reserved teachers) to teach denominational RE.	School must follow the LA Agreed Syllabus unless the parents request a denominational one. Foundation governors have rights in the appointment of staff (called reserved teachers) to teach denominational RE.
Membership of governing body	Church (foundation) governors have a majority of two over all other governors. The parish priest is usually *ex officio* a member of the governing body. All governors combine to elect the Chair. A proportion of foundation governors must also be parent governors.	Church (foundation) governors are in a minority. The parish priest is usually *ex officio* a member of the governing body. All governors combine to elect the Chair.	Church (foundation) governors are in a minority. The parish priest is usually *ex officio* a member of the governing body. All governors combine to elect the Chair.

	Voluntary aided	Voluntary controlled	Foundation
Funding	LA Local Management of Schools (LMS)) formula. The governors' 10 per cent liability for capital works met from locally raised fund, PCCs, local and diocesan trusts. DFC interest may also be used when available.	LA LMS formula.	LA LMS formula.
Admissions	Governors determine the policy and make the decisions but must comply with national guidelines. They must consult the LA and all other schools in the area each year (or every other year if conditions met).	The LA is responsible for admission, but must consult the governing body each year.	Governors determine the policy and make the decisions but must comply with national guidelines. They must consult the LA and all other schools in the area each year (or every other year if conditions met).
Advice	LA Director of Education (or equivalent) has certain rights to attend governor meetings to give advice. Diocesan Directors of Education have parallel rights.	LA Director of Education (or equivalent) has certain rights to attend governor meetings to give advice. Governors may give similar rights to the Diocesan Director of Education.	LA Director of Education (or equivalent) has certain rights to attend governor meetings to give advice. Governors may give similar rights to the Diocesan Director of Education.
Inspection	Ofsted inspectors look at most issues. SIAS inspectors inspect RE, worship, ethos, and leadership and management.	Ofsted inspectors look at general issues and RE. SIAS inspectors inspect worship, ethos, and leadership and management.	Ofsted inspectors look at general issues and RE. SIAS inspectors inspect worship, ethos, and leadership and management.

More than
Caring and
Sharing

An ethos statement for a church school

Recognising its historic foundation, the school will preserve and develop its religious character in accordance with the principles of the Church at parish and diocesan level.

The school aims to serve its community by providing education of the highest quality within the context of Christian belief and practice. It encourages an understanding of the meaning and significance of faith and promotes Christian values through the experience of all its pupils.

More than Caring and Sharing

Expectations of a church school

As a minimum, every church school should:

- ensure the school is led by a head teacher committed, with the help of the staff, to establishing and maintaining the Christian character of the school in its day-to-day activities and in the curriculum;
- engage meaningfully in an effective act of Christian worship every day;
- offer a school life that incorporates the values of the Christian faith;
- provide a Christian understanding of the world and the place of humanity within it, reflected in worship and the everyday life of the school;
- work within a framework of discipline that demonstrates a readiness to seek and offer forgiveness;
- have an explicit commitment to honesty and openness;
- begin to share the Christian hope and experience that the greatest power in life and beyond it is selfless love;
- provide a knowledge of how to pray and of the liturgy, respecting those of other faiths who cannot in conscience engage in the full liturgy of Christian worship;
- provide an awareness of the challenge of the spiritual life within everyday experience;
- respect the beliefs of others and of other faiths, but be confident

in its own faith, not actively seeking to convert children from the faith of their parents, but providing an experience of what it is to live in a community that celebrates the Christian faith. The school should promote a sense of inclusion and involve the leaders of other faiths as appropriate;

- celebrate the identity and nature of culturally and ethnically diverse groups;
- ensure that religious education is given in at least 5 per cent of school time and that the character and quality of religious education are particular concerns of the head teacher and governing body;
- observe the major Christian festivals and, where other faiths are present, ensure that those faiths are able and encouraged to mark their major festivals with integrity;
- maintain and develop an active and affirming relationship with the parish church(es);
- proclaim that it is a church school on its external signboard and on its stationery, and make appropriate use of Christian symbols inside and outside the school.

(Adapted from *The Way Ahead: Church of England Schools in the New Millennium*, Church House Publishing, 2001).